SPRINGER SERIES
IN PERCEPTION ENGINEERING

Series Editor: Ramesh C. Jain

Springer Series
in Perception Engineering

John M. Gauch

Multiresolution Image Shape Description

With 45 Illustrations

Springer-Verlag
New York Berlin Heidelberg London Paris
Tokyo Hong Kong Barcelona Budapest

John M. Gauch
College of Computer Science
Northeastern University
Boston, MA 02115
USA

Series Editor

Ramesh C. Jain
Electrical Engineering and
   Computer Science Department
University of Michigan
Ann Arbor, MI 48109
USA

Library of Congress Cataloging-in-Publication Data
Gauch, John M.
     Multiresolution image shape description / John M. Gauch.
        p.   cm.—(Springer series in perception engineering)
     Revision of the author's thesis (Ph.D.)—University of North
Carolina at Chapel Hill, 1989.
     Includes bibliographical references.

        ISBN-13: 978-1-4612-7689-0   e-ISBN-13: 978-1-4612-2832-5
        DOI: 10.1007/978-1-4612-2832-5

     1. Image processing.   I. Title.   II. Series.
TA1632.G38   1991
621.36′7—dc20   91-31356

Printed on acid-free paper.

Production managed by Bill Imbornoni; manufacturing supervised by Robert Paella.
Typeset by Asco Trade Typesetting Ltd., Hong Kong.

9 8 7 6 5 4 3 2 1

Preface

Much of our understanding of the relationships among geometric structures in images is based on the shape of these structures and their relative orientations, positions and sizes. Thus, developing quantitative methods for capturing shape information from digital images is an important area for computer vision research. This book describes the theory, implementation, and application of two multiresolution image shape description methods. The author begins by motivating the need for quantitative methods for describing both the spatial and intensity variations of structures in grey-scale images. Two new methods which capture this information are then developed. The first, the intensity axis of symmetry, is a collection of branching and bending surfaces which correspond to the skeleton of the image. The second method, multiresolution vertex curves, focuses on surface curvature properties as the image is blurred by a sequence of Gaussian filters. Implementation techniques for these image shape descriptions are described in detail. Surface functionals are minimized subject to symmetry constraints to obtain the intensity axis of symmetry. Robust numerical methods are developed for calculating and following vertex curves through scale space. Finally, the author demonstrates how grey-scale images can be segmented into geometrically coherent regions using these shape description techniques. Building quantitative analysis applications in terms of these visually sensible image regions promises to be an exciting area of biomedical computer vision research.

Acknowledgments

This book is a corrected and revised version of the author's Ph.D. dissertation, *The Multiresolution Intensity Axis of Symmetry and its Application to Image Segmentation*, completed at the University of North Carolina at Chapel Hill, NC, in 1989.

The author owes a great debt of gratitude to the five members of the dissertation committee. This research was supervised by Stephen Pizer, whose patience, knowledge, enthusiasm, and financial support made this work possible. The author also wishes to thank James Coggins and Robert Gardner for their careful reading of the dissertation and their many helpful comments. Paul Jaques and Frederick Brooks, Jr., contributed their own valuable insights to the problems addressed in this book which are also greatly appreciated.

The author also thanks fellow graduate students in the graphics and image lab at the University of North Carolina for numerous fruitful conversations. In particular, Tim Cullip, Graham Gash, Andrew Glassner, Chen-Hong Hsieh, Mark Levoy, Larry Lifshitz, and Bill Oliver, together with the faculty, staff, and other students, have made Chapel Hill an exciting place to conduct computer vision research.

Special thanks are due to my wife Susan for her continual understanding, her hard work keeping us both on track to graduate together, and especially for bringing our daughter Laura into the world. This book is dedicated to Susan.

John M. Gauch

Contents

CHAPTER 1

Introduction and Background

Quantitative analysis is the primary motivation for digital image processing in many applications. For example, locating and measuring anatomical structures in medical images is an important first step in diagnosis and treatment planning. In biology and other scientific disciplines, the
analysis of structures in images often leads to better understanding of the
underlying mechanisms in the systems being studied. Often the shape of
structures within images plays an important role in this identification and
analysis process. For example, we might distinguish different types of
blood cells by their shape and perhaps gain an understanding of blood
disorders by an analysis of shape variations. For this reason, determining
how the shape of image structures should be best represented to facilitate
quantitative analysis is one of the central problems in computer-aided
image analysis. To answer this difficult question requires an understanding of what shape is and how shape information should be extracted from
grey-scale images.

There is an important distinction between object shape and image
shape. Object shape traditionally involves all aspects of an object except
its position, orientation and size. For example, a triangle is still "triangle
shaped" no matter how it is positioned, oriented or scaled. Extending the
notion of shape to images requires invariance to similar transformations
in the intensity dimension. Thus, image shape involves all aspects of an
image except its position, orientation, size, mean grey level, and intensity
scale factor. For example, an intensity ramp (which is bright on one side
and gradually becomes dark on the other side) is "ramp shaped" independent of what the maximum and minimum intensities in the grey-scale
image are so long as intensity varies linearly as we move down the
ramp. For more complex images, shape involves the spatial and intensity
branching and bending of structures in images and their geometric relationships. Since we are interested in identifying and studying sensible
geometric structures in grey-scale medical images, our attention is
focused on developing methods for describing the shape of structures in
grey-scale images and the relationships between these structures. Two
classic approaches have been employed to achieve this goal.

The first class of methods begins by partitioning the image into segments (collections of pixels which belong to the same object in the image)
and then describes the shape of the resulting image regions. Image segmentation is an active area of research and beyond the scope of this work
(see [Blicher, 1985]). Instead, we focus our attention on methods devised

to describe the shape of these pre-defined objects. The second approach for describing image structures is to capture properties of the grey-scale image directly. These methods have the advantage of not requiring an image segmentation, although they often lead to segmentation, yet they often run into difficulty when they attempt to describe the shape of image objects. The next two sections review representative methods for describing the shape of pre-defined objects and for describing features of the grey-scale images.

1.1. Shape Description

To describe object shape, we are interested in everything about the object except its position, orientation and size. For example, a triangle is still "triangle shaped" no matter how it is positioned, oriented, or scaled. Representations of objects which are invariant to changes in position, orientation, and scale are called *object shape descriptions*. The following are methods for describing the shape of predefined objects.

One of the simplest descriptions of predefined objects is based on swept surfaces. When a disk is swept along a path in three dimensions, we get a three-dimensional volume called a *generalized cylinder* [Binford, 1971]. If the size and orientation of the disk varies along the path, the result is a *generalized cone* [Nevatia and Binford, 1977]. This notion has also been applied to derive a representation of two-dimensional objects. When line segments are swept along a path in two dimensions, the result is a shape description called *generalized ribbons* [Rosenfeld, 1984]. This idea has not been extended to grey-scale images nor to multiple resolutions. Generalized cones have been used as a shape description for image generation and also for object recognition [Agin, 1972; Soroka and Bajcsy, 1976; Soroka, 1979; Shani, 1980; Brooks, 1981]. A serious problem with this approach is the difficulty in establishing the axis direction and cross-section behavior, particularly in the presence of image noise and distortion. For this reason, more recent axis-based shape description methods show more promise.

If all possible lines connecting a fixed point on the boundary of an object to another point on the boundary are considered, those lines which have the same angle of intersection with the boundary tangent at both endpoints form a special subset of line segments called *local symme-*

tries. When the locus of all midpoints of local symmetry lines are combined, the result is an axis called the *smoothed local symmetry* (SLS). The radius and curvature of this axis can be characterized to obtain a shape description for two-dimensional binary images [Brady and Asada, 1984]. One problem with this representation is that the axis segments describing a connected object are not guaranteed to be connected. Extensions to two-dimensional grey-scale images and to multiresolution hierarchies may be possible but have not been investigated.

The *symmetric axis* (SA), also known as the *skeleton* or *medial axis*, is a shape description which characterizes the spine along the middle of an object [Blum, 1974]. More specifically, the SA is the locus of centers of maximal tangent circles inside (or outside) the object. These points form connected axes which describe the branching structure of the object. Associated with each axis is a radius function which records how wide the object is at every point on the axis and a curvature function which describes how the axis is bending. These functions together can be used to characterize shapes. This method was originally devised to handle two-dimensional binary images [Blum and Nagel, 1978], but it has been extended to three-dimensional binary images [Nackman, 1982]. The calculation of an approximate two-dimensional symmetric axis from two-dimensional grey-scale images has also been investigated [Wang, Wu and Rosenfeld, 1981]. The major problem with this shape description is its sensitivity to noise in the boundary. To overcome this difficulty, multiresolution techniques have been applied to two-dimensional binary images to determine the significance of axis branches and to impose a scale-based relationship on axis segments [Dill, 1987; Pizer, 1987]. These noise handling methods have also been extended to three-dimensional images [Bloomberg, 1988].

The set of all midpoints of shorter interboundary arcs of maximal circles tangent to the boundary of an object defines a shape description called the *process inferred symmetry axis* (PISA) [Leyton, 1986]. This axis is similar to the SLS and SA except that each axis segment is associated with a process of deformation (such as denting in, bulging out) which operates on the object boundary. In this way, the shape of an object can be described by the sequence of deformations which transforms a primordial object into the object being described. While this is an exciting approach, it has not yet been extended to handle image noise and has been defined only for two-dimensional binary images.

When we inscribe a circle in a triangle and then use an affine transformation to deform the triangle, the circle is deformed into an ellipse. The principal axes of this ellipse give us the principal strains of the deformation. By extending this notion to describe the movement of a collection of landmarks on the boundary of an object, the result is a deformation representation for two-dimensional binary images called the *homology map* [Bookstein, 1986]. Like the PISA approach, the homology map could be used to describe the shape of an object by the deformation required to transform a given primordial object. How this method responds to image noise is not known. It is also unknown how effectively this technique can be used as a shape descriptor for three-dimensional images or two-dimensional grey-scale images.

One way to study the shape of a predefined object is to focus on the curvature of its boundary. If an object's boundary is decomposed into sections bounded by two adjacent curvature minima, curve segments called *codons* are obtained [Richards and Hoffman, 1985]. Each codon contains a single curvature maximum and can be classified into five types, depending on the signs of the three curvature extrema. By considering sections bounded by two adjacent curvature maxima, we obtain five *codon duals*, which can be classified by simply changing the sign and type of each curvature extremum in our codon classification [Leyton, 1986]. The shape characterization provided by codons is sensitive to boundary noise and has not been extended from two-dimensional binary images to other image types.

1.2. Image Description

There are a multitude of image features which can be computed directly from the grey-scale values in an image and characterize the image in some way. Simple examples include the location of edges, ridges, valleys, maxima, or minima in an image. We call such representations *image descriptions*. The following are image description methods which capture interesting image properties.

When a two-dimensional grey-scale image is viewed as a surface in three dimensions, one natural geographical subdivision is into *hills* and *dales* [Cayley, 1859; Maxwell, 1870]. If this is extended further to include ridge lines (which separate dales) and course lines (which separate hills), the surface can be partitioned into *slope districts*, (areas which have a single hill top and dale bottom in common). If the critical points on the surface (hill tops, dale bottoms and saddle points) are connected in a graph by ridge and course lines, the *critical point configuration graph* is obtained [Nackman, 1984]. This image description method has recently been used to characterize two-dimensional grey-scale images. It is very sensitive to noise and also ignores almost all information about the shape of the hills and dales.

The *Smale diagram* is another image representation which partitions an image surface into regions [Smale, 1967]. In this case, the isointensity contours through the saddle points of the image are used to represent the extent of bright and dark regions in the image. The nesting of these curves can then be represented in a graph and used to characterize the nesting of bright and dark regions in the image [Blicher, 1985]. This method has several problems. As with slope districts, it is very sensitive to image noise, and all information about the intensity shape of the individual regions is lost in this representation. Also, the relative positions of nested contours are not retained by this description.

The *image pyramid* is one of the earliest multiresolution image representations. It is so called because it consists of multiple versions of the image which when stacked on each other form a pyramid. The bottom of the pyramid is the original image. Each intermediate level in the pyramid is a 2^n by 2^n image with pixel values found by averaging four pixels in the 2^{n+1} by 2^{n+1} image directly below it in the pyramid. The top of this pyramid is a one pixel image containing the average intensity in the original image. This method provides noise-insensitive descriptions of grey-scale images which have been applied with some success to several applications, for example, edge detection [Kelly, 1971], hierarchical template matching [Rosenfeld, 1977], and image segmentation [Burt and Hong, 1981]. The major shortcomings of this approach are the aliasing caused by the ad hoc nature in which lower resolution images are computed and the difficulty of following image features from level to level.

Another multiresolution representation for grey-scale images is called the *difference of low pass transform* (DOLP) [Crowley and Parker, 1984]. The first step in calculating the DOLP is convolving the original image with a sequence of bandpass filters (where each filter is the difference of two low pass filters). This results in a stack of images called the *Laplacian stack* [Marr and Poggio, 1980]. Since the Laplacian is equal to the trace of the Hessian, it captures an important aspect of the behavior of the second derivative of the image. A second phase of locating peaks and following ridges in this three-dimensional structure yields a graph-like representation of the grey-scale image. While this graph describes the hierarchical nature of bar-like regions in the image, the shape of these regions is not explicitly incorporated.

The *intensity stack* is an image description designed to address the theoretical issues in multiresolution image analysis [Koenderink, 1984]. Like the pyramid, it consists of a stack of images at decreasing resolutions. Unlike the pyramid, the intensity stack uses Gaussian blurring to obtain this collection of images in order to guarantee that no new extrema are generated as we blur. Therefore it is possible to follow the paths of intensity extrema (local maxima and minima) from one resolution to the next. As the blurring increases, each of the non-extremal points is associated with one of these extremal paths. This yields a hierarchical (tree-like) description of light and dark regions in the image which can be used for image segmentation [Lifshitz, 1987]. While the shape of these extremal paths is not described explicitly, these paths capture scale information in the image.

The *Gaussian derivative n-jet* is a generalization of the intensity stack which captures the changes in the first n derivatives of the image under blurring. One effective method for calculating the n-jet which avoids numerical differentiation is to precalculate the first n derivatives of the Gaussian blurring kernel and apply these to the input image [Koenderink, 1987]. Another effective method for calculating this representation uses differences of offset Gaussians (DOOGs) to approximate these derivatives [Young, 1986]. The n-jet is robust against image noise and represents the differential geometry of the image but does not directly yield a structural description of the image. Efforts to extract geometric image features from the n-jet are under investigation and show great promise [Blom, 1988].

1.3. Image Shape Description

The many shape and image descriptions described above share one goal in common. They attempt to abstract the image in order to extract some useful information about the structure of an object or an image. The first class of methods describes the shape properties of predefined objects while the second class of methods focuses on features which can be directly calculated from images. Our objective is to combine these two ideas to obtain a shape description which can be applied directly to images. We will show that the shape of structures in grey-scale images can effectively be described in terms of the shape of the level sets for the image and that the structural relationships between image structures can be determined by examining the image at multiple resolutions or scales.

The shape description method which provides the best structural decomposition of objects into connected components is the symmetric axis. The image description that best captures the hierarchical relationships between image structures is the intensity stack. To combine these desirable properties in one image representation requires extending the symmetric axis to grey scale images and using multiresolution analysis to identify the hierarchical relationships between individual components of this new symmetry axis. To demonstrate the viability of this approach, we have designed and implemented a new image shape description called the *intensity axis of symmetry* (IAS) and an associated curvature based description called *vertex curves*. Both of these descriptions focus on properties of individual level curves and combine this information across intensities to obtain representations which capture both spatial and intensity properties of shapes in the image. To demonstrate the effectiveness of our shape description method, we have implemented an interactive image segmentation program which identifies and displays visually sensible image regions associated with individual components of the IAS.

Our shape description approach has three major advantages over other methods:

1. The image segmentation step required to define objects before describing their shape will no longer be necessary. This is particularly important because image segmentation is a difficult task.

2. Geometric relationships among many image features are directly captured by the structural properties of an image shape description. For example, a shape description which identifies the intensity ridges in an image will also describe the adjacency relationship between the intensity maxima on these ridges. This will allow image analysis applications to identify and study image regions which are geometrically related, without requiring a priori semantic knowledge of the image geometry.

3. Geometric coherence can be used to identify image regions which are

visually sensible. Thus, shape-based image segmentation is possible once you have a representation of image shape.

Now we turn our attention to the issues involved in designing and implementing an image shape representation which accomplishes these objectives. In Chapter 2 introduce and describe the theoretical properties of the intensity axis of symmetry. Methods for computing this image shape description are discussed in Chapter 3. Shape-based image segmentation is described in Chapter 4. In Chapter 5 we introduce vertex curves and use this curvature-based shape description method to study the multiresolution properties of the intensity axis of symmetry. Conclusions and directions for future research are the subject of Chapter 6.

CHAPTER 2

The Intensity Axis of Symmetry

The previous chapter reviewed existing shape and image description methods and identified the symmetric axis and the intensity stack as the most promising methods in these respective categories. This chapter defines a new image shape description called the intensity axis of symmetry (IAS) which shares the advantages of both these methods. This is accomplished by describing simultaneously the shape of the whole collection of level curves which comprise the image. A discussion of the important descriptive properties of the IAS then follows.

2.1. Axes of Symmetry

Disks are perfectly symmetrical. Hence, it is natural to use disks to somehow describe the symmetry of predefined objects. One way to do this is to derive axes of symmetry based on the properties of disks tangent to the boundary of an object. At mentioned in Chapter 1, several methods use this approach. The locus of midpoints of chords of tangent disks are used to define smoothed local symmetries (SLS) [Brady and Asada, 1984]. The locus of midpoints of arcs of tangent disks are used to define process inferred symmetry axes (PISA) [Leyton, 1986]. Finally, the locus of centers of tangent disks are used to define the symmetric axis (SA) [Blum, 1974]. When the radius of each of these disks is also recorded, the result is the *symmetric axis transform* (SAT) [Blum and Nagel, 1978].

How the tangent disk is positioned relative to the object boundary distinguishes three classes of SA. The *internal* SA is defined by centers of maximal (doubly tangent) disks which are entirely within the object while the *external* SA is defined by centers of maximal disks which are entirely outside the object. The *global* SA is defined by the centers of all doubly tangent disks, even those which intersect the object boundary. By focusing on either the internal or external SA, the shape of the object or the "hole" not filled by the object can be represented. Using the global SA, all object symmetries can be represented.

The SA has many attractive properties. First, the branching structure of the object is reflected by the branching of the axis. This yields a natural correspondence between components of the object and components of the shape description. Second, the bending and flaring of the object is reflected by changes in the curvature of the axis and of the radius of the tangent disks. This gives us a way to compare and contrast similar shapes. Finally, this shape description is unique and with the radius information can be used to recreate the object.

One of the problems with the SA is that it is very sensitive. Noise and small detail in the object boundary can cause large but "unimportant" branches to appear in the axis. These confound shape analysis by introducing large numbers of axis segments and by breaking up main branches into numerous small sections. One solution is to use multiple resolution analysis to derive a hierarchy on the individual components of the shape description. This approach yields the *multiresolution symmetric axis* [Pizer, 1986]. Computing this shape description involves measuring the importance of each branch in the symmetric axis. As the resolution decreases, objects tend to simplify, eventually becoming ellipses. Because the symmetric axis varies smoothly with the figure it represents, the branching structure of the axis also simplifies as resolution is lowered. Thus, we can follow axis branches to annihilation through a multiple resolution sequence of object boundaries. The importance of each branch is then determined by its annihilation resolution.

The order of annihilation of axis branches can be used to impose a hierarchy on axis branches (see Figure 2.1). When a branch annihilates, the two remaining adjacent branches combine to form a single branch, and the annihilated branch is labeled as a sub-object of this new branch. When we do this for all axis branches, the result is a description which reflects the shape of an object and also the hierarchy of sub-objects which

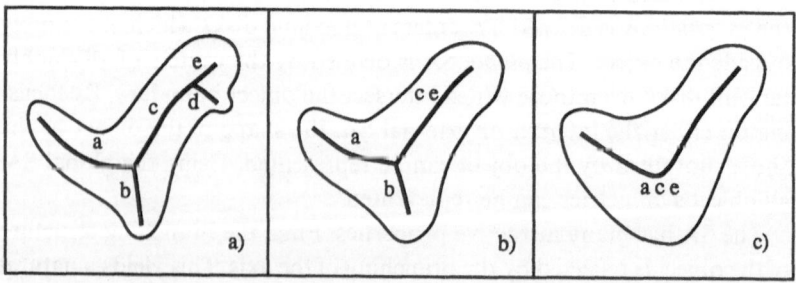

FIGURE 2.1. Branching hierarchy imposed on the symmetric axis by resolution reduction (from left to right). When axis segment "d" annihilates it is labeled as a sub-branch of a new composite branch "ce." Later, when axis "b" annihilates it is labeled as a sub-branch of the major axis "ace."

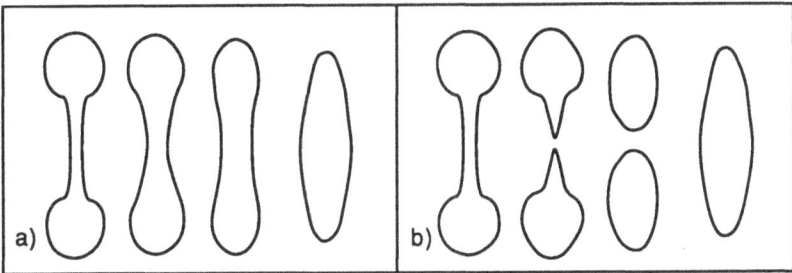

FIGURE 2.2. Three stages of boundary blurring (left) and figure blurring (right).

make up the object. This multiresolution shape description can then be used to study image structure as a function of scale.

To obtain a multiresolution sequence of object boundaries, the two natural alternatives are boundary blurring and figure blurring (see Figure 2.2). Both techniques yield acceptable results but are suited to different problems. When boundary blurring is used, object topology is maintained but figural similarity is frequently not preserved; two shapes with different topologies may be visually similar at one scale yet appear quite different at another scale. This similarity problem can be avoided by blurring the object figure. When the characteristic function representing the object figure is convolved with a Gaussian, it yields a grey-scale image. The blurred object boundary can then be obtained by selecting one of the intensity level curves of this image. One natural method is to select the intensity level curve which preserves the object's area. As with any choice, this can result in topological changes in the boundary as resolution is reduced. Thus, visual similarity is maintained at the expense of boundary topology.

The problem of selecting a single level curve to represent the boundary of a figure-blurred object leads to an important observation. Binary images are special cases of grey-scale images; they are images which have only two grey values. Thus, binary images should be treated as grey-scale images and grey-scale shape descriptions should be applied to describe such images. To preserve causality under resolution reduction, Gaussian blurring of the intensities should be used to impose a multiresolution hierarchy on this description [Koenderink, 1984]. This further motivates the investigation of grey-scale shape descriptions.

2.2. The Intensity Axis of Symmetry (IAS)

The objective of this section is to generalize the symmetric axis to describe grey-scale images. Two-dimensional grey-scale images can be viewed as a surface in three space defined by the graph $(x, y, I(x, y))$. One way to describe the shape of such graphs is to use the tools of differential geometry to describe the surface. An alternative is to describe the two regions of space separated by this surface. The major problem with either of these approaches is that the intensity dimension is incommensurate with the spatial dimensions. There is no natural choice as to what intensity change is equivalent to what spatial distance. Shape descriptions which vary with a particular choice of equivalency must therefore be avoided. This problem can be overcome by describing image shape in terms of the level sets of the image (see Figure 2.3). These curves are by definition restricted to a single intensity, so the shape of these curves will not vary if image intensity is uniformly rescaled.

The level sets for a two-dimensional grey-scale image are the planar curves defined by $I(x, y) = L$, for all intensities L in the image. These level sets create boundaries that partition each level into an inside and an outside. The image surface is the union of its level sets at their respective intensity levels. The volume below the surface consists of all points (x, y, I)

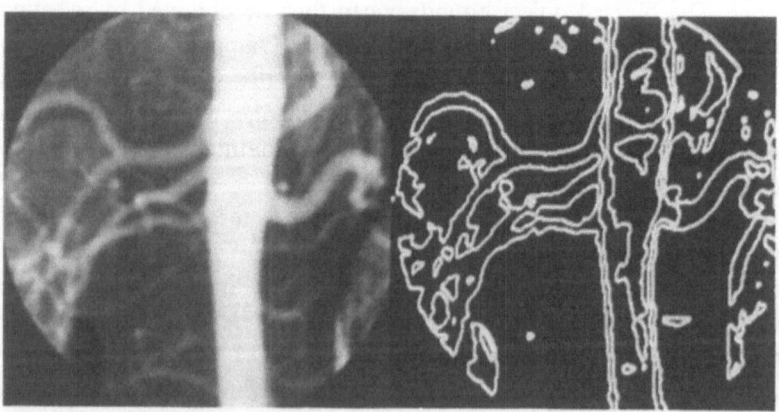

FIGURE 2.3. A digital subtraction angiogram (DSA) image of blood vessels (left) and a collection of selected intensity level curves (right).

which have $I < I(x, y)$, while the volume above the image surface consists of all points where $I > I(x, y)$. Thus, it is possible to represent the image surface and the regions on either side of the surface in terms of the level curves or regions defined by level curves. To describe the shape of each of these level curves, we use the symmetric axis transform.

By calculating the SA for each level curve L and embedding these axes in three dimensions at their respective intensity levels, the result is a grey-scale shape description called the IAS. When the axis branches are defined according to multiresolution analysis and the scale of individual axis branches is calculated and recorded, the result is the *multiresolution* IAS. What does this collection of axis transforms describe? Because each of the level curves of the graph $(x, y, I(x, y))$ partition each level into an inside and an outside, we can describe two things. The volume below the image surface can be represented by the internal symmetric axis transform for each level. Since image intensity corresponds to the height of the image surface, this volume can be used to describe the shape of light structures in the image. Similarly, the volume above the image surface can be represented by the external symmetric axis transform for each level and can be used to describe the shape of dark regions in the image. The union of the internal and external symmetric axis transforms combines this information to describe the shape of light and dark structures in the image simultaneously.

2.3. Properties of the IAS

One of the strengths of the symmetric axis transform is its ability to represent the shape of individual components of an object and combine this information to describe the shape of the whole object. To understand how the IAS behaves in this regard requires an analysis of the following:

1. the topology of the basic elements of the IAS,
2. the bending and branching behavior of these structures,
3. the behavior of the radius function for these structures,
4. the one-to-one mapping between objects and axis transforms,
5. the invariance of the IAS under image rotation, translation, and uniform scaling.

These five topics are discussed in the following sections. To simplify the analysis, it is assumed that the original intensity function $I(x, y)$ is smooth and continuously differentiable, and that the critical points of this function are generic (isolated and non-degenerate) and can be catalogued and studied using Morse theory [Morse, 1934].

2.3.1. Axis Topology

The first step in understanding the IAS is identifying the basic elements which comprise this shape description. This can be accomplished by examining the behavior of level curves. Assuming that the image $I(x, y)$ is smooth and continuous, the curves defined by $I(x, y) = L$ will vary smoothly with intensity L except at critical points. Because the symmetric axis varies smoothly with the region it represents, the collection of axes for these level curves will vary smoothly with L and form smooth branching surfaces in three dimensions (see Figure 2.4). We call these surfaces IAS *axis sheets* or simply *axis sheets*.

At critical points, the topology of level curves changes abruptly but in a manner which can be easily analyzed. At local extrema, level curves reduce to a point and then disappear (depending on the intensity direction from which the extremum is approached). At saddle points, level curves come together, cross and then come apart again. The IAS near these regions also changes abruptly. The remainder of this section investi-

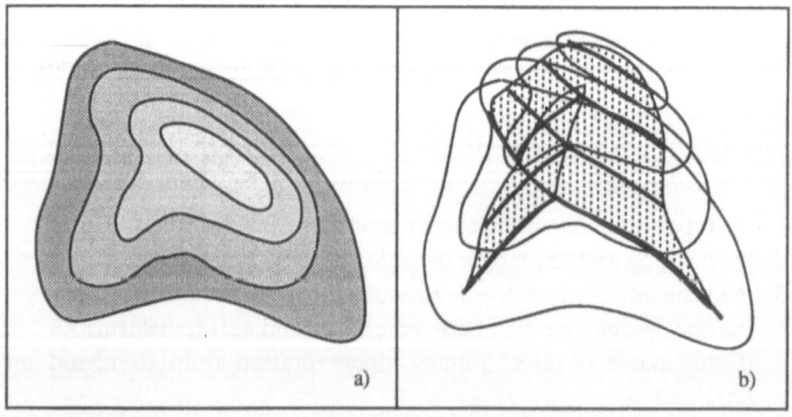

FIGURE 2.4. The level curves (left) and corresponding IAS (right) for part of a synthetic image. The shaded branching surfaces are called axis sheets.

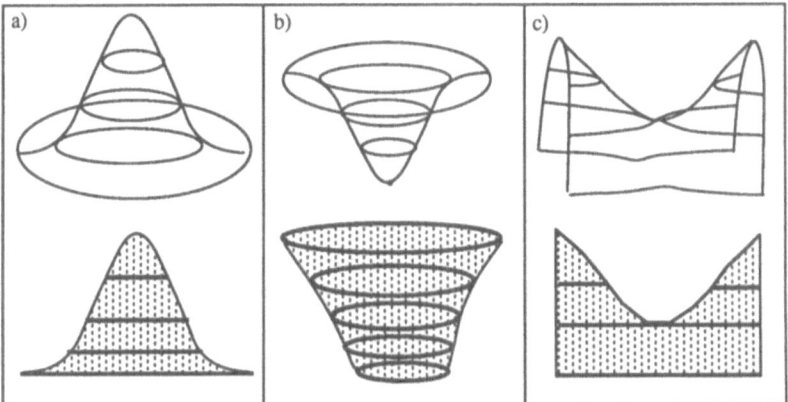

FIGURE 2.5. IAS behavior near critical points in the image illustrating a) the level curves near an intensity maximum and the corresponding sheet termination in the IAS, b) the level curves near an intensity minimum and the corresponding loop termination in the IAS, c) the level curves near an intensity saddle point and the corresponding axis tear in the IAS. In each case, the IAS sheets are shaded and displaced below the image surface. In addition, the SAs for the selected level curves are shown in bold for emphasis.

gates axis sheet behavior near critical points and the indications of shape this behavior provides.

At a local maximum the axis sheet for the region under the image surface shrinks with the level curve until it disappears at the critical point. The axis sheet above the surface near a local minimum behaves similarly. These points are called *sheet terminations* (see Figure 2.5a). They are an indication of locally lightest or darkest spots in the image. The behavior of sheets on the opposite side of the image surface near these extrema is more complicated. Consider what happens to the symmetric axis for an object with a hole, as the hole gradually shrinks and then disappears. Initially, the axis for the object loops around the hole. This loop shrinks slightly as the hole shrinks, but suddenly disappears when the hole disappears. At the same time, a new piece of axis down the center of the object appears. This is exactly the situation we observe near local extrema in an image. If we look at the IAS just above a local minimum, we find that an axis sheet forms a loop around the indentation near the minimum and that this loop disappears and another axis sheet appears as we move below the extremum. Similar axis behavior is also observed for the IAS above the surface near a local maximum. These changes in IAS sheets are called *loop terminations* (see Figure 2.5b). They give us an indication of the nesting of dark regions within light regions and vice versa.

The level curves near a saddle point cross each other. If we calculate the IAS for the region under the image surface near such crossing points, we find that the axis sheet separates into two pieces at the saddle point as we move up in intensity. These are called *axis tears* (see Figure 2.5c). The same behavior is observed for the IAS above the image surface except that the sheets tear apart as we go down in intensity. Thus, we call saddle points *tear points* of the IAS. These points are special for two other reasons. First, level curves through saddle points describe the nesting of hills and pits in the image [Blicher, 1985]. Thus, the axis sheets can be partitioned at these levels to obtain descriptions of local light and dark regions of the image. Second, saddle points are the only points in common to the IASs of both polarities, so they act as connection points between the IAS below the surface and the IAS above the surface. This adds coherence to our shape description which can be exploited to describe the relationship between local light and dark regions in the image.

2.3.2. Axis Bending and Branching

While critical point behavior yields a basic understanding of the relationships between light and dark regions in the image, additional information about the spatial and intensity shape of these regions is conveyed by the branching and bending of IAS sheets. How individual sheets bend gives an indication of the shape of the corresponding light and dark regions of the image. How these sheets combine to form branching surfaces captures the global branching structure of the image being described. By combining these shape properties, it is possible to describe the basic shape of the grey-scale image.

The bending of axis sheets reflects two different image properties. When the bending is in the spatial dimensions, it captures how ridges (or valleys) in the image are bending. When the bending is in the intensity dimension, it reflects the asymmetry of intensity ridge (or valley) profiles (see Figure 2.6). To quantify this bending requires that the curvature at each point on the axis sheets be calculated in two directions. If the normal to the axis sheet at the point (x', y', i') is given by some vector $\mathbf{N} = (x, y, i)$,

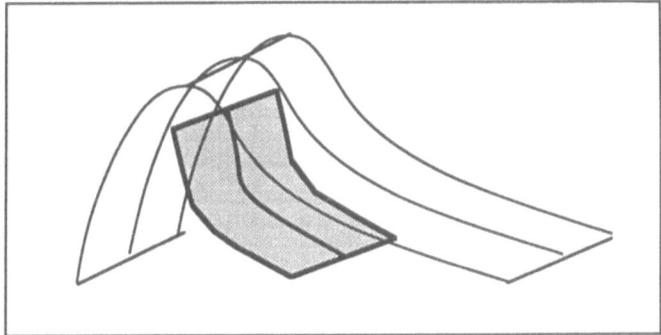

FIGURE 2.6. Axis bending properties in the intensity dimension. One side of this ridge corresponds to a steep edge while the opposite side slopes more gently.

then the axis tangent in the spatial dimensions will be perpendicular to this normal yet have no intensity component. This tangent vector is given by $T_1 = (-y, x, 0)$. The axis tangent in the orthogonal direction will be the direction on the axis surface where intensity changes most rapidly. This tangent to the axis surface is given by $T_2 = N \times T_1 = (-iy, -ix, x^2 + y^2)$. Spatial bending is reflected by axis curvature in the T_1 direction while intensity bending is indicated by axis curvature in the T_2 direction. The derivatives of these curvature functions measure how this bending changes as we move along the axis. As with the two-dimensional and three-dimensional SA, these curvature properties can be used to characterize the shape of sections of individual axis sheets.

Once we have a description of the shape of individual sheets, we need to consider how these sheets are connected. Recall that the SA for an object consists of a collection of axis curves connected at axis branch points. Similarly, the IAS consists of axis surfaces connected by *branch curves*. The branching structure of IAS sheets above and below the image surface reflect the spatial relationships between dark and light regions in the image respectively. Each light ridge-like structure in the grey-scale image is described by an axis sheet below the image surface. The connections between the axis sheets reflect the connections between these intensity ridges in the image. Similarly, the branching of each dark valley-like structure in the image is described by IAS sheet connections above the image surface.

The branching of IAS sheets is most easily visualized for image regions

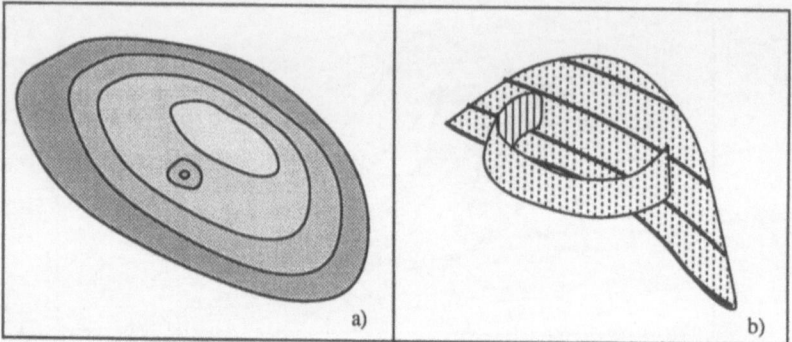

FIGURE 2.7. Axis branching near an intensity minimum on the side of a ridge. The SAs for the selected level curves in a) are shown in bold on the IAS surfaces in b).

which correspond to ridges on hillsides (see Figure 2.4). Here, a single axis sheet corresponding to the ridge is attached to the IAS sheet describing the hillside. When many ridges and subridges are involved, the branching of the IAS reflects the hierarchical relationships among these image structures. Because local intensity extrema introduce loops in the IAS, the axis sheets are not connected in a pure hierarchy. The axis sheets which make up these loops will be connected by two separate branch curves to other axis sheets (see Figure 2.7). These two-ended connections require additional data structures to record the relationships between axis sheets. This issue is described in detail in Chapter 5.

2.3.3. Axis Radius Function

In addition to capturing the bending and branching of light and dark regions of an image, the IAS also reflects width properties of image structures. Recall that each point on the SAT has associated with it the radius of the maximal disk at that point. This function describes the widening and narrowing of individual axis branches. Extending this notion to the intensity dimension, each point on the IAS has associated with it the radius of the maximal disk at that point and within that level curve. Thus, the radius function on the IAS reflects the spatial width of structures in the image. Changes in this radius function along axis sheets yield additional information about the shape of structures in the grey-scale image.

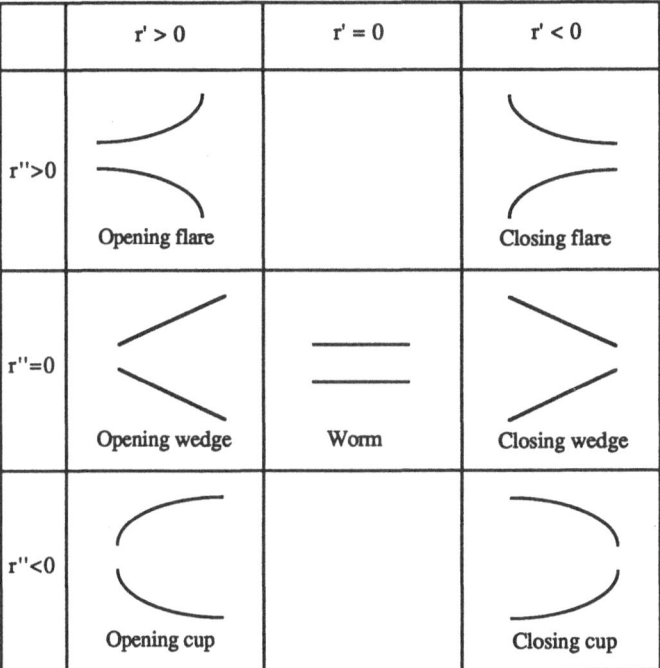

	r' > 0	r' = 0	r' < 0
r''>0	Opening flare		Closing flare
r''=0	Opening wedge	Worm	Closing wedge
r''<0	Opening cup		Closing cup

FIGURE 2.8. Widening and narrowing properties of the SA characterized by the first and second derivative behavior of the radius function in the spatial dimension [Blum and Nagel, 1978].

Width changes in the spatial dimensions reflect the widening or narrowing of intensity ridges and valleys. This occurs when the first derivative of the radius function in the direction of the spatial tangent T_1 (defined above) is positive or negative respectively. The second derivative behavior in the same direction describes the flaring and cupping of ridges and valleys. The seven combinations of these derivative properties correspond to those for the radius function of the two-dimensional symmetric axis (see Figure 2.8).

The sharpness and roundness of ridges or valleys corresponds to width changes in the intensity dimension. Consider the radius function as we follow the intensity tangent T_2 (defined above) up the axis sheet for a ridge. Because the image surface is described by a function, the radius decreases monotonically as we move toward higher intensities. Hence,

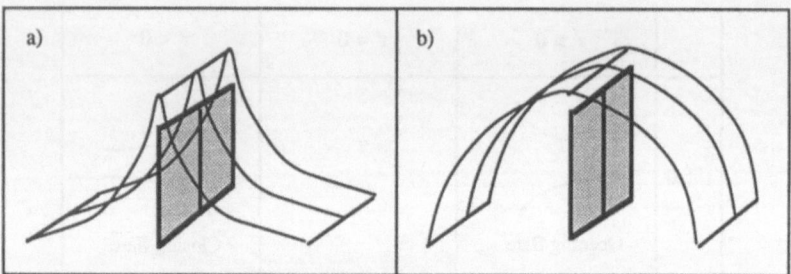

FIGURE 2.9. Roundness properties determined by the second derivative behavior of the radius function in the intensity direction. The second derivative is positive as we go up the axis for the ridge on the left and negative for the ridge on the right.

the first derivative is always negative. When the second derivative in the T_2 direction is also negative, the ridge appears round at the top. Conversely, ridges which appear sharp have a positive second derivative (see Figure 2.9). This analysis extends to valleys by considering the radius function as we go down the sheet corresponding to the valley. When the shape properties provided by the radius function are combined with the other properties we have described, we obtain an overall description of the shape of a two-dimensional grey-scale image.

2.3.4. Axis Inverse Mapping

In addition to describing the width properties of image structures, the radius function described above provides the necessary information to recreate the original image given the IAS. This is best illustrated by considering an axis point on the two-dimensional SA. The radius of the maximal disk at that point is given by the radius function. By drawing the maximal disk centered at that point, we define the region of the figure associated with that point on the axis. Extending this notion to all of the points on a SA branch, the union of all maximal disks centered on the axis branch defines the region of the object associated with the selected SA branch. When the union of all maximal disks on all branches is computed, the result is the original two-dimensional object. The SA with its associated radius function is called a *transform* because this inverse mapping exists.

Extending this inverse mapping to the IAS is straightforward. The

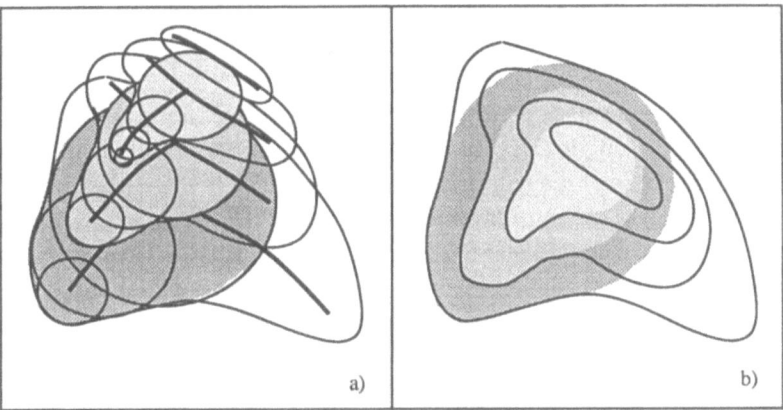

FIGURE 2.10. Associating an object region with a single IAS sheet. The union of maximal disks at their respective intensity levels on the axis sheet (left) defines an intensity volume. The maximum intensity at each (x, y) point of this volume defines the object region associated with this IAS sheet (right).

volume associated with an axis sheet is defined to be the union of all maximal disks for all points on the sheet at their respective intensity levels (see Figure 2.10). By considering the volume associated with all internal IAS sheets, the result is the volume under the image surface $(x, y, I(x, y))$. The original intensity image can then be recovered by simply recording the maximal intensity value at each (x, y) position. Thus, the internal IAS plus the radius function also defines a transform. Similarly, the external IAS defines the volume above the image surface whose minimal values at each (x, y) position give the original image. This inverse mapping property of the IAS is very important in the image segmentation applications discussed in Chapter 4.

2.3.5. Axis Invariance

Now that the descriptive properties of the IAS have been identified, one major property remains to be verified. Recall that image shape descriptions were originally defined to be representations of images which are independent of "position, orientation, size, mean grey value, and intensity scale factor." To demonstrate that the IAS satisfies these requirements it must be shown that the IAS remains invariant to changes in spatial coordinates corresponding to rotations, translations, and uniform scalings. In addition, IAS invariance to changes of the intensity scale factor and mean grey value must be demonstrated.

Image transformations which consist only of rotations and translations preserve length. Because the IAS is defined in terms of the locus of centers of maximal tangent disks, the relative sizes of these disks will be unchanged by such transformations. Hence, the relative locations of axis points will not change if an image is rotated or translated. Thus, the effect of rotating and translating the image is to rotate and translate the IAS by an equal amount. Because distance is preserved, the radius function along these transformed axis sheets also remains unchanged. One of the important reasons for using curvature to describe curves and surfaces is that these curvature functions remain invariant to affine changes of coordinates (such as rotations and translations). Consequently, axis curvature in both the spatial and intensity directions remains invariant to image rotations and translations. Hence, all aspects of the IAS remain invariant to image rotations and translations.

Image transformations which involve uniform spatial scalings do not preserve length. Such transformations alter the relative positions of the locus of centers of maximal disks defining the IAS. As a consequence, the radius and curvature functions of the IAS change by some scale factor, while the structure of the branching remains the same. While this scale factor can be easily derived from the Jacobian of the transformation mapping when it is known, the more general situation of calculating scale-invariant shape descriptions for images when the image transformation is unknown is more complex and has not been incorporated into the present definition of the IAS. Thus, the IAS is invariant to rotations and translations but not fully to uniform spatial scalings.

The IAS is defined in terms of the behavior of a family of image level curves. The intensity value associated with these curves does not affect any aspect of the two dimensional SAs for these curves, nor does it alter how these SAs connect from level to level. Thus, the basic structure of the IAS and its radius function remain invariant to changes in intensity scale factor and mean grey value. The same is not true for the IAS curvature function. Since the surface derivatives in the intensity dimension are measured relative to the image intensity scale, IAS curvature function, which is calculated in terms of these derivatives, will vary with changes in the image intensity scale factor. Thus, only measurements of intensity bending are affected by intensity scale manipulations; all other aspects of the IAS are unchanged.

2.4. Discussion

By focusing on the shape of the level curves defined by a grey-scale image, the intensity axis of symmetry represents the image exactly and has many useful properties as a shape description for grey-scale images. It provides a means for identifying individual image structures and a mechanism for studying the shape characteristics of these structures and geometrical relationships between these structures. Thus, the IAS provides a very powerful tool for image description. The next task is to demonstrate an effective means of computing the IAS for discrete grey-scale images.

CHAPTER 3

Computing the Intensity Axis of Symmetry

The previous chapter defined the intensity axis of symmetry (IAS) and described certain desirable properties of this image shape description. This chapter describes our approach for calculating a discrete representation of the IAS given an arbitrary grey scale image. The emphasis is on calculating an accurate and robust approximation of the IAS; questions of efficiency are of secondary interest here and will be discussed only briefly.

3.1. Level by Level Calculation of Axes

While it is natural to describe the IAS in terms of the symmetry axis (SA) for a collection of binary images, there are several inherent problems with using this approach to calculate the IAS. In medical applications, it is common for images to contain 12 or more bits of data per pixel. Thus, many slices would be necessary to represent image structures accurately, making the time to calculate the SAs for the whole image excessive. More seriously, the boundaries of these binary images change topology as intensity varies. This makes it difficult to connect contours or axes from slice to slice. Finally, when discrete binary images are used to calculate SAs, artifacts due to aliasing are introduced which complicate the following of SAs from slice to slice. These problems together make it almost impossible to calculate the IAS on a slice-by-slice basis. Therefore, a method which processes all intensity levels in the image simultaneously has been developed.

3.2. Simultaneous Calculation of Axes

To develop an algorithm for calculating the IAS which processes all intensity levels simultaneously requires an image model which provides spatial and intensity coherence. The *active contour model* [Kass, 1987] uses a curve-based functional to provide a spatially coherent model of closed contours. By extending this functional to surfaces, a new image representation called the *active surface model* is defined which provides coherence across both space and intensity levels. By selecting the appropriate initial conditions and minimizing this surface functional, it is possible to solve for the entire IAS structure simultaneously.

The initial position of the active surface should reflect the basic structure of the IAS. Since the original image viewed as a surface in (x, y, I) captures the basic topology of the level curves used to define the IAS, this surface is used as the starting position of the IAS. By defining a function of (x, y, I) which reflects the symmetry of the image at each location and intensity level in the image, the active surface can be "attracted" towards the intensity axis of symmetry. Partitioning the active surface into patches which correspond to the individual sheets of the IAS can then be accomplished by determining the links from each point on the active surface to the point which was attracted to the same location from the "opposite" direction. These axis sheets can then be displayed or used for further shape analysis.

3.2.1. A Review of the Active Contour Model

The active contour model, as originally specified, provides a technique for fitting closed curves to edges, ridges and other image features while maintaining smoothness constraints on the curve. These constraints are based on first and second derivative properties of the curve and ensure that the solution is relatively insensitive to noisy image features. The key to this technique is the minimization of the energy functional

$$\text{Energy} = \int \left[w_1 \| f_s(s) \|^2 + w_2 \| f_{ss}(s) \|^2 + g(f(s)) \right] ds$$

where $f(s) = (x(s), y(s))$ are the coordinates of the curve parameterized by arc length s, and first and second partial derivatives of the curve with respect to arc length s are denoted with subscripts. The weights w_1 and w_2 control the effects of these derivatives and enable us to specify the curve behavior. When w_1 is less than w_2, the curve resembles a spline; otherwise it resembles a membrane. The third term in this functional is used to direct the active contour towards the image features of interest. For example, to fit the active contour to the boundary of an object, the function $g(f(s))$ should reflect edge strengths in the input image. To solve for the curve $f(s)$ which minimizes this energy functional, Kass developed discrete formulations of the two Euler equations associated with this functional. These equations are solved iteratively for $x(s)$ and $y(s)$.

3.2.2. The Active Surface Model

Extending the active contour model to surfaces requires an energy functional defined on surfaces with terms capturing the first and second derivative properties of the surface. To allow the greatest flexibility in controlling the parametric surface given by

$$f(u,v) = (x(u,v), y(u,v), I(u,v)),$$

the active contour energy functional is extended to a two-dimensional surface as follows:

$$\text{Energy} = \iint \left[w_1 \| f_u(u,v) \|^2 + w_2 \| f_v(u,v) \|^2 + w_3 \| f_{uu}(u,v) \|^2 \right.$$
$$\left. + w_4 \| f_{uv}(u,v) \|^2 + w_5 \| f_{vv}(u,v) \|^2 + g(f(u,v)) \right] du\, dv$$

where u and v are the parametric coordinates of the surface, and the first and second partial derivatives of the surface in these directions are denoted by subscripts. The five weights w_i control the effects of these partial derivatives and enable us to specify the surface behavior to resemble a spline or a flexible membrane. The attraction of the surface by image features, here symmetry, is given by the function $g(f(u,v))$.

While curves with several hundred points can be solved using the Euler equations developed by Kass, the surfaces we are dealing with consist of tens of thousands of points. Thus, simultaneous solution via Euler equations becomes unreasonable, and iterative relaxation techniques are more practical. In the MIN_SURFACE program, each point p on the active surface is examined on each iteration of this relaxation process to see if any of the neighbors of p have a lower contribution to the total energy than p. If so, p is moved to its neighbor's location. Since the attraction function $g(f(u,v))$ does not have local minima other than the global minimum, this gradient descent minimization technique yields a surface representing the IAS after a finite number of iterations. Several implementation issues are of interest here.

CONSTRAINING THE MOVEMENT OF THE ACTIVE SURFACE

The first and second partial derivatives of the parameterized surface in the functional above consist of sums of squares of the partial derivatives of the individual coordinate functions. For example, the first derivative of the parameterized surface with respect to u is given by

$$\| f_u(u, v) \|^2 = x_u(u, v)^2 + y_u(u, v)^2 + I_u(u, v)^2.$$

Thus, the active surface described so far treats the intensity and spatial dimensions equally. This poses several problems. First, there is no obvious way to relate energy in the spatial dimensions to energy in the intensity dimension. Even if this could be overcome by some type of image normalization, a more serious problem must be addressed. The basic shape of the image is reflected in the number and positions of hills and pits in the image and in the structure of the ridges and valleys which connect these extrema. If the behavior of the active surface is unconstrained, the minimal functional could yield an approximation of the IAS which does not have the same basic structure as the image. For example, if the active surface is very stiff, the resulting IAS could have fewer extremal points than the original image. This is a fundamental problem which must be avoided.

This problem is solved by constraining the movement of points on the active surface and by selecting an appropriate starting position for the surface. The iterative minimization technique described above considers the nearest neighbors of a point in its search for lower energy contributions. In three dimensions, these neighbors lie in a $3 \times 3 \times 3$ cube, so there are 26 nearest neighbors of the central point. By restricting this search to points of the same intensity value, 18 of these 26 nearest neighbors are excluded from this search. This forces the active surface to move only in the spatial dimensions, leaving the intensity structure of the surface untouched. With this constraint on the active surface, it is clear that the original image should be used as the starting position of the active surface in order to ensure that the resulting IAS will have the same number of extrema and the same connectivity structure between extrema as the input image.

REPRESENTING THE ACTIVE SURFACE

Because the calculation is to produce a discrete IAS for a discrete input image, the most practical representation of the IAS is a discrete sampling of the $x(u, v)$, $y(u, v)$ and $I(u, v)$ functions. This can be viewed as a function of three variables (u, v, C), where C represents one of the three coordinate functions of the IAS (x, y, I). This three-dimensional function is represented as a matrix of integer values and stored in an image using the /usr/image format [Zimmerman, 1981]. The $(u, v, 0)$ and $(u, v, 1)$ entries in this image give the (x, y) coordinates of the IAS point while the $(u, v, 2)$ entry gives the intensity value I at this point.

One advantage of this representation is that the existing /usr/image display tools can be used to study the coordinates of the IAS to gain a better understanding of the IAS surface and the behavior of the MIN_SURFACE program. More importantly, the IAS can be stored and accessed in a uniform and convenient manner by the programs which process this shape description. Because the input and output of the MIN_SURFACE program are in the same format, it is possible to take the output after N iterations, inspect the results, and use this intermediate surface as input for another M iterations.

SELECTING THE PARTIAL DERIVATIVE WEIGHTS

The weights w_i on the partial derivatives in the energy functional specify the internal constraints on the active surface. Increasing the relative contribution of the first order derivatives in the energy functional introduces a penalty associated with the rate of change of the surface in space. This penalty is reduced when the surface area is minimized, causing the surface to behave more like a flexible membrane similar to a soap bubble. By increasing the relative contribution of the second order terms, a penalty is introduced whenever the first order terms change abruptly. This penalty is reduced when the number and sharpness of corners are minimized and when the sample points on the active surface are uniformly spaced, causing the surface to behave more like a spline. The contribution of the symmetry function $g(f(u, v))$ in the energy functional has an implicit weight of one. Thus, the absolute values of the partial derivative weights control how much the surface is internally constrained versus externally attracted towards the IAS.

After experimenting with several combinations of these weights, we concluded that the active surface most successfully converges on the IAS when its behavior is more like a flexible membrane than like a spline. This allows the surface to have sharp folds at the tops of axis sheets and where axis sheets branch. After experimenting with the absolute value of these weights, we found that the following weights provide a reasonable balance between the internal and external constraints:

$$w_1 = 0.2, \quad w_2 = 0.2, \quad w_3 = 0.1, \quad w_4 = 0.1, \quad w_5 = 0.1.$$

The number of medical images used for these experiments was fairly small (six) and of limited variety, so these weights may not be ideal for every grey scale image. Finding the "best" weights for every situation is beyond the scope of our research.

ESTIMATING THE PARTIAL DERIVATIVES OF THE SURFACE

The partial derivatives of points on the surface are calculated using symmetric finite differences to avoid any particular bias in the movement of the surface. The formulas used in the active surface program are

$$x_u(u, v) = (x(u + 1, v) - x(u - 1, v))/2$$

$$x_v(u, v) = (x(u, v + 1) - x(u, v - 1))/2$$

$$x_{uu}(u, v) = (x(u + 1, v) - 2x(u, v) + x(u - 1, v))$$

$$x_{uv}(u, v) = (x(u + 1, v + 1) - x(u - 1, v + 1) - x(u + 1, v - 1)$$
$$+ x(u - 1, v - 1))/4$$

$$x_{vv}(u, v) = (x(u, v + 1) - 2x(u, v) + x(u, v - 1))$$

with similar equations for $y(u, v)$. Since the active surface is restricted to move only in the x and y dimensions, the partial derivatives of intensity $I(u, v)$ with respect to u and v will not change. Therefore, these terms will cancel when calculating the change in functional energy when a point is moved in (x, y). Hence, there is no need to calculate the partial derivatives of $I(u, v)$.

Some care must be taken at the boundaries of the surface where the neighbors of a pixel may be out of bounds. The solution chosen was to clip the indices of the point's neighbors to lie within $[u_{min}, u_{max}]$ and $[v_{min}, v_{max}]$. For example, if (u, v) is a boundary pixel where $u - 1 < u_{min}$, we use u_{min} in place of $u - 1$ when calculating neighboring values of x and y. The effect is to extend the image with a copy of the extreme rows and columns in each direction. The values of the boundary pixels will be repeated in some of the partial derivative calculations, but this was deemed a better solution than either wrapping around the indices or ignoring the out of bounds pixels in the calculations.

DETERMINING THE OVERALL CHANGE IN THE ENERGY FUNCTIONAL
FOR A GIVEN POINT MOVEMENT

The estimates of surface partial derivatives are weighted and integrated with the image feature contribution $g(f(u, v))$ over the active surface to obtain an estimate of the total energy of the functional. To minimize this energy, the eight neighbors of the point (x, y, I) in the spatial dimensions are checked to see if a movement of the active surface to one of these neighbors will reduce the total energy. If so, the point is moved. The tricky aspect of this calculation is determining the effect of this movement on each neighbor's energy term without the undue computation involved in recalculating the energy contribution of all eight neighbors.

By inspecting the finite differences above, it is clear that only some of the partial derivatives of these neighbors are changed when the point (x, y, I) goes to the point (x', y', I). The 28 energy terms to be recalculated are summarized below.

a. For the points $(u - 1, v)$ and $(u + 1, v)$ the new values of the partial derivatives x_u, x_{uu}, y_u, and y_{uu}, are recalculated.
b. For the points $(u, v - 1)$ and $(u, v + 1)$ the new values of the partial derivatives x_v, x_{vv}, y_v, and y_{vv} are recalculated.
c. For the points $(u - 1, v - 1)$, and $(u - 1, v + 1)$, $(u + 1, v - 1)$ and $(u + 1, v + 1)$ the new values of the partial derivatives x_{uv} and y_{uv} are recalculated.
d. For the point (u, v) the new values of the partial derivatives x_{uu}, x_{vv}, y_{uu}, and y_{vv} are calculated.

Thus, the work involved in checking the eight neighbors of a given point on the surface involves calculating $28 \times 8 = 224$ new partial derivatives. This is a considerable savings over the $90 \times 8 = 720$ calculations required by the brute force approach and produces much better results than simply ignoring the contribution of the point's eight neighbors to the energy functional.

STOPPING THIS ITERATIVE PROCESS ONCE THE SURFACE HAS CONVERGED

There are several natural ways to determine when the active surface has converged to the IAS. One alternative is to stop the iterative process when the number of iterations reaches some predefined limit. For example, if we consider the maximum distance a point must travel to reach the symmetry axis, the iteration limit should be at least one half the image width divided by the step size. This termination condition does not reflect the structure of the image being processed and is usually too high.

We really want the stopping condition to reflect the "change" in the active surface from one iteration to the next. One alternative is to stop when the total energy change falls below some given threshold. Another alternative is to say that the active surface has converged when the number of points moved in an iteration falls below a specified threshold. Both of these approaches have potential problems. If the solution is globally good but bad in isolated areas, the surface may be far from the correct solution in these isolated areas, yet the energy change or the number of moving points may fall below their respective thresholds. The problem of setting these thresholds is further complicated by the fact that the rate of change of the active surface may vary from image to image.

Making the stopping criteria depend on the image is attractive for pragmatic reasons. For this study, we will use this approach and watch for cases where problems might arise. The thresholds most effective for calculating the IAS for medical images are (1) an iteration threshold of about 25% of the image width, and (2) a threshold on the number of moving pixels of about 1% of the total number of pixels in the input image. These threshold values are input parameters of the MIN_SURFACE program. For a typical 256×256 medical image the active surface requires about 50 iterations before meeting the stopping criteria indicating approximate convergence to the IAS.

3.2.3. The Image Symmetry Function

Because the SA is defined in terms of the centers of maximal disks, the distance from an axis point to the nearest boundary point is locally maximal; a small step in either direction perpendicular to the axis towards the object boundary will result in a lower distance to the boundary. This distance function reflects the symmetry of the object and together with an active contour originating on the object boundary can be used to compute the two-dimensional SA for the object (see Figure 3.1).

A distance function can also be used to identify points on the IAS. By computing the distance from each point (x, y, I) to the nearest point (x', y', I) on the image surface at the same intensity level, it is possible to define an *image symmetry function* which reflects the size of the largest tangent disk that can be centered at every point. When the weight controlling the contribution of the image symmetry function in the active surface functional above is negative, minimizing this functional will cause the active surface to converge to points with maximal distance to the image surface. Since these points correspond to the centers of maximal disks tangent to the level curves of the image, this symmetry function

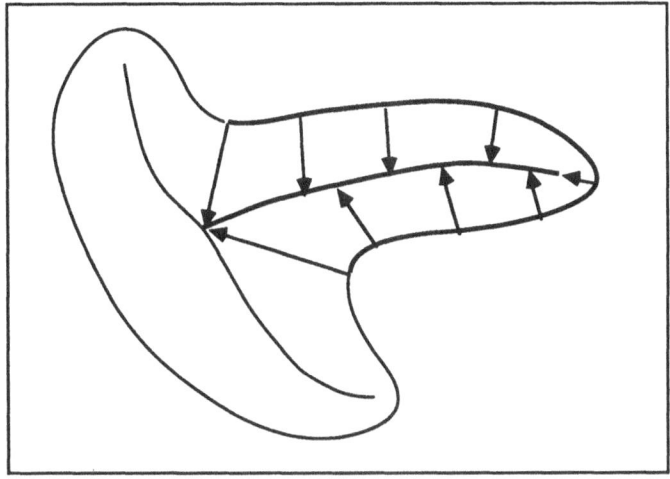

FIGURE 3.1. A portion of an object's boundary attracted by the symmetry function to one branch of the two-dimensional symmetric axis of the object.

directs the active surface towards the IAS. To effectively compute the image symmetry function, several implementation issues must be addressed.

REPRESENTING THE IMAGE SYMMETRY FUNCTION

Because the function $g(x, y, I)$ will be used extensively and is costly to compute, the values of this function are precalculated and recorded in a three-dimensional array which is stored as an image in the /usr/image format. Because sub-pixel accuracy is not needed by the active surface program, the sampling grid in x and y corresponds to the original image sampling rate. The sampling in the intensity dimension is another matter. Considering the space and time requirements, it seems unreasonable to calculate $g(x, y, I)$ for every intensity level in the image. Experience shows that quite satisfactory results are possible by selecting 50 evenly spaced intensity levels and calculating the image symmetry function for those levels.

CALCULATING THE IMAGE SYMMETRY FUNCTION

Two algorithms have been implemented for calculating the function $g(x, y, I)$. The first uses a brute force search which is slow but accurate. It involves computing the spatial distance from the point (x, y) to every other pixel (x', y') in the image. This distance is compared with the current distance value recorded at position (x, y, I') in the image symmetry table, where I' is the intensity of the pixel (x', y'). If the new distance is less than the current value at (x, y, I') in the table, the new minimum at that intensity is saved. Thus, the distance to the nearest point on the image surface at every intensity is computed for every point in (x, y, I). This algorithm requires $O(n^4)$ time, where n is the image width, and requires $O(n^2 r)$ space for an image intensity range of r values. This is far too slow, so a faster method of computing the symmetry function was developed.

The second algorithm is directly based on the grass fire analogy described above. The grey scale image is thresholded at r evenly-spaced intensity levels to produce a collection of binary images. Here, the 1-valued pixels are inside these level curves and correspond to grass, while the 0-valued pixels are outside these level curves and correspond to "burned" grass. The effect of burning grass for one unit of time is simulated by removing all 1-valued pixels which have 0-valued neighbors (i.e., the boundary pixels of these binary images). This "burning" can be accomplished by scanning the image once by rows and again by columns. The time each pixel is removed is recorded in the output image. After a limited number of iterations, all 1-valued pixels are removed and their removal times provide an accurate estimate of the symmetry function for the selected intensity levels. This algorithm requires $O(n^3 r)$ time for images of $n \times n$ pixels thresholded at r intensity values. This is a significant improvement over the first algorithm since r is usually much less than n and because numerical calculations are not required to calculate distances.

3.2.4. Linking the Active Surface

Before the branching behavior of the IAS sheets can be used to investigate the spatial relationships between structures in the image, the active surface must be partitioned into the individual axis sheets which comprise the IAS for the image. The strategy here is to identify the two portions of the active surface which are attracted by the image symmetry function to "opposite" sides of each IAS sheet. These two patches of the active surface represent two sections of the grass fire whose quench points define the IAS sheet.

The first step in this partitioning process involves linking each point on the active surface to the point which was attracted to the same location from the "opposite" direction. Using these links, it is possible to use region growing to identify the two patches of active surface which converge from "opposite" directions and form each axis sheet. By joining these patches, the basic topological difference between the IAS and the active surface (a sheet versus two sides of a folded surface) can be eliminated. Before computing these links, a more precise definition of what is meant by "opposite" is needed.

Recall that the grass fire analogy defines IAS points as the quench points of a grass fire started at the boundary of an object. These quench points are where the fires have arrived from two (or more) different directions simultaneously and put each other out (since grass can not burn twice). Hence, the burning time from these points on the boundary to the quench point are identical. Since time is proportional to distance in this model, this means that there are two (or more) points on the boundary of the object which share the same minimal distance from the boundary to the quench point. These points on the boundary are called *involutes*. The objectives of the linking program are (1) finding and linking the involutes of the active surface and (2) representing this information so other analysis programs can make use of these links. Several implementation issues are of interest here.

DETERMINING IF TWO POINTS ARE INVOLUTES

After attraction to the IAS, the spatial location of involutes in (x, y, I) should be identical. Since the discrete sampling of the active surface makes this unlikely, we use closeness in (x, y, I) to define the involutes of points on the active surface. In particular, if the coordinates of a point (u, v) are (x, y, I), the involute of this point is the active surface point (u', v') with coordinates (x', y', I') such that the distance $\|(x, y, I) - (x', y', I')\|$ is minimal.

One problem with this discrete definition of involutes is that it is asymmetrical. The reason is that the involute of each active surface point is determined independently according to the distance minimization above. Hence, the involute of the point (u', v') above could be some active surface point other than (u, v) which is closer to (x', y', I') In addition, it is possible for two or more points on the active surface to share the same involute. To avoid consequent problems, the algorithms which use involute information have been designed so that they do not require symmetrical identification of involutes.

A second problem with this approach is that the points on the active surface adjacent to (u, v) are likely to be attracted to points near (x, y, I). Thus, we place an additional restriction on involutes. The surface distance $\|(u, v) - (u', v')\|$ between two involutes must be above a specified threshold. Satisfactory results are achieved by setting this threshold so that the eight nearest neighbors of (u, v) are excluded as potential involutes. One situation where this heuristic introduces some problems is near the end curves of IAS sheets. Since points on these end curves correspond to SA endpoints, these points quench themselves due to the higher order contact of the maximal disk to the level curve at these points. Therefore, the assignment of involutes for such points may be inaccurate using this method. Rather than attempting to detect IAS end curves using some other mechanism, the algorithms which use involute information have been designed to be robust to these potential misassignments.

FINDING THE LINKS CONNECTING INVOLUTES

Three algorithms have been implemented for calculating the links connecting involutes on the active surface. The first method uses brute force searching. For each point on the active surface (u, v), the distance in (x, y, I) from that point to every other point (u', v') on the active surface is calculated and the minimal distance is recorded in a link table. The coordinates (u', v') of the closest point are also recorded for future use. As noted above, the nearest neighbors of (u, v) are excluded from this search. This method produces accurate results but is computationally very expensive. For an image with width n, $O(n^4)$ distance calculations are required, each of which involves several multiplications and divisions. As a result, several hours of CPU time on a 10 MIPS workstation are required to calculate the links for a 256×256 image.

To improve this situation, a second method was devised. Because the values of (x, y, I) on the active surface are integer-valued and restricted to a specified range, it is possible to use a variation on bucket sorting to calculate the involutes of the points on the active surface. The first step in this process is to allocate buckets corresponding to each of the possible (x, y, I) coordinates of points on the active surface. The next step involves distributing the original (u, v) coordinates of surface points into their corresponding (x, y, I) buckets. The buckets can contain several points.

Thus if two or more points share the same (x, y, I) position, they will fall in the same bucket. The last step is to search for the closest point in (x, y, I) for each point on the active surface. The distribution of points into buckets greatly reduces the time required for this search. If the bucket for the point (u, v) has two or more points, the linking is trivial and involves no searching. If only one entry has fallen in the (x, y, I) bucket corresponding to the point (u, v), then the neighboring buckets in (x, y, I) are searched until a non-empty bucket is found. The (u', v') coordinates of the closest point give the coordinates of the involute in this case. To avoid problems near IAS branch curves and end curves, the nearest neighbors of (u, v) are again excluded from this search. While this algorithm is more complex than the brute force search method, it is much faster and produces identical results.

To improve the quality of the links between involutes on the active surface, a third method was implemented. Noting the requirement that involutes share the same minimal distance from the boundary to the quench point, Cullip [Cullip, 1989] suggested a heuristic for identifying involutes which minimizes a weighted sum of three terms to find the most likely links. The expression for the linking error for the points (u, v) at (x, y, I) and (u', v') at (x', y', I') is given by

$$w_1 \|(x, y, I) - (x', y', I')\| - w_2 \|(u, v) - (u', v')\|$$
$$+ w_3 | \|(x, y) - (u, v)\| - \|(x', y') - (u', v')\| |.$$

The first term reflects the spatial distance between two points on the active surface in (x, y, I) coordinates. When this term is minimized, the two points quench at the same location. The second term measures the parametric distance between these points on the active surface. This term should be maximized to avoid linking adjacent points on the active surface to each other. The third term reflects the difference between the *quenching distances* of the two points. The quenching distance is the distance a point travels from its initial position on the image boundary (u, v) to its quenching point (x, y, I). Hence, this term should be minimized to identify the most likely involutes. The weights w_i control the relative contribution of these three terms. Reasonable results are achieved with the weights $w_1 = 1$, $w_2 = 1$, and $w_3 = 1$. Finding the "best" weights for every situation was beyond the scope of our research but may result in even better identification of involutes.

The output of all link finding programs is a matrix of (u', v', d) values giving the surface coordinates of the involute of the point (u, v) and the distance d between these two points. This data is stored as a three-dimensional image in /usr/image format to ensure that the data is accessible in a uniform and convenient manner by other IAS analysis and display programs. The indices of this image are (u, v, L) where u and v are the coordinates of the active surface and L indexes one of the three components of the (u', v', d) link. Thus, the $(u, v, 0)$ and $(u, v, 1)$ entries of this image give the (u', v') coordinates of the involute for (u, v) while the $(u, v, 2)$ entry contains the distance d between these points. This representation together with the three-dimensional image representing the (x, y, I) coordinates of the points on the active surface provide a concise representation of the IAS shape description.

3.2.5. Identifying Individual Axis Sheets

In order to investigate the branching behavior of the IAS, the active surface must first be partitioned into the individual axis sheets which comprise the IAS for the image. Because it is difficult to identify and connect the points on the surface which correspond to IAS branch curves and IAS end curves, methods which rely on the identification of these points to partition the active surface into axis sheets will be very error prone. On the other hand, the links between involutes calculated above make it easy to identify which pairs of points are on the same axis sheet. Using this information, a special region growing algorithm was developed for identifying the set of points on the active surface which make up each of the IAS sheets. Issues addressed in the implementation of this algorithm are discussed below.

If we are given a starting point on the active surface, what other points lie on the same IAS sheet? By definition, the involute of this point has been attracted to the same (x, y, I) location as the starting point. Therefore, the involute belongs on the same IAS sheet. Extending this notion to small neighborhoods called *patches* on the active surface, we find that the patch which includes the starting point and the patch which includes the involute are also attracted to nearby (x, y, I) locations. Thus, the neighborhoods of the starting point and the quench point are also on the same sheet. When the patches become larger and the neighborhoods include IAS branch curves or IAS end curves, the situation becomes more complex.

Because active surface points on either side of an IAS branch curve lie on different axis sheets, these branch points should act as a boundary to stop the neighborhood from including points from both of these adjacent axis sheets. Thus, points should be iteratively added to these neighborhood patches only if (1) they are a nearest neighbor of one of the existing points in the patch and (2) their involute is either a member of the involute patch or one of the nearest neighbors of the involute patch. These constraints prevent patches from growing beyond IAS branch curves (see Figure 3.2). Thus, all of the points on the same IAS axis sheet can be found by growing the neighborhood patches for the starting point and its involute until both patches are stable. The union of these points defines the active surface region associated with a single IAS sheet.

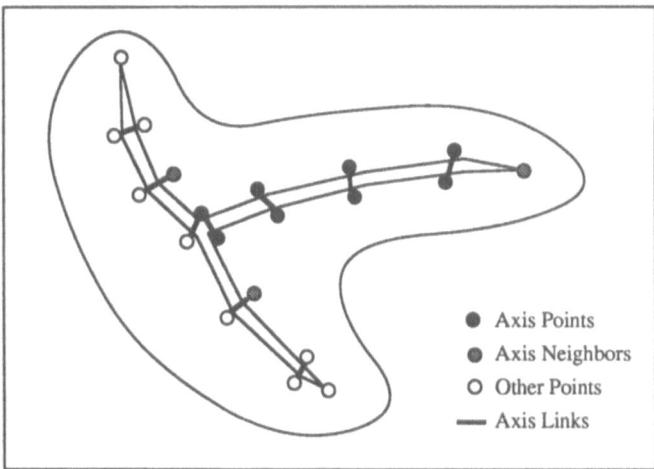

FIGURE 3.2. Linking involutes to identify the set of points on a single axis of the two-dimensional symmetric axis. The points in black belong to a single branch. The shaded points are the neighbors of this branch. Other SA points are white.

REPRESENTING AN ACTIVE SURFACE REGION

The two patches of involute points which define an active surface region can be represented as two non-intersecting sets of (u, v) coordinates. These two sets are initialized with the coordinates of the seed point and its involute respectively.

As the region growing algorithm proceeds, it is necessary to record the coordinates of the neighboring pixels of these two patches. This introduces two additional sets of (u, v) coordinates. The coordinates of these neighboring pixels are recalculated after each iteration and used in the region growing algorithm described above.

To facilitate fast set lookup, the regions associated with these four non-overlapping sets of points are recorded in a two-dimensional array and stored as a grey-scale image in /usr/image format. Here, predefined set identifiers are used to determine which of the four sets each (u, v) point belongs to. The 0-valued pixels belong to no set. Thus, to see if a given (u, v) point is a member of a particular set requires only an array lookup and a comparison.

DISPLAYING AN ACTIVE SURFACE REGION

One method for visualizing an active surface region is to display the region image described above. This provides useful structural information, but the context of the region within the image is lost. A more attractive alternative is to use the region image as a display mask for the original image. Here, the original image intensities are displayed where region pixels are non-zero, and black is displayed elsewhere. To test this algorithm, we implemented an interactive program on a color workstation which allows the user to select starting points using the mouse. These seeds are used to calculate the set of points which make up the active surface region for the selected IAS sheet. The masking technique described above is used to display this region in an adjacent image.

In a large number of cases, the resulting regions correspond to sensible image structures or parts of these structures (see Figure 3.3). Unfortunately, these regions occasionally subsume each other. For example, one starting point may yield part of an image structure while a nearby starting point produces a larger region which includes the former region. This undesirable behavior may be caused by the selection of starting points

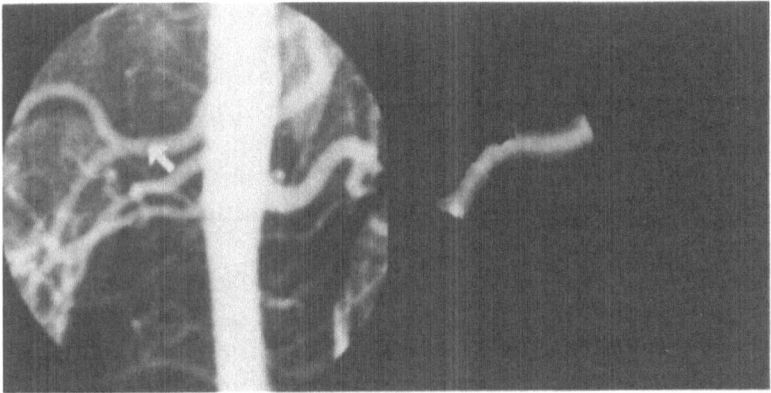

FIGURE 3.3 A digital subtraction angiogram (DSA) image and an active surface region corresponding to a sensible image structure.

near IAS branch curves, but the true cause has not been identified. To avoid this problem, a second algorithm was devised which partitions the entire active surface into nonoverlapping regions corresponding to all of the individual axis sheets comprising the IAS.

CALCULATING THE IAS PARTITION

The interactive region-growing algorithm often produces excellent results, but what is really needed is a partitioning of the whole active surface into N regions corresponding to the N axis sheets which make up the IAS. The selection of an appropriate seed for each axis sheet is not straightforward. It is natural to expect the same region to be grown if any point inside the region is used as a seed, but this is not always the case. Occasionally, when points on the region boundary or near an axis end curve are selected as seeds, only a subset of the larger "true" region is obtained. These artifacts are due to discreteness problems in the linking of involutes and the sequential nature of the region growing algorithm. The problem of finding the "correct" seeds is avoided by considering a large number of seeds, calculating the associated regions, and identifying for each point on the active surface the largest region which includes that point. These are called the *maximal regions* of the active surface.

The simplest method to identify the largest region which includes a given point (u, v) is to grow all possible active surface regions, determine which regions include (u, v) and record the region identifier for the region which has the largest area. By considering each point on the active surface separately, this brute force algorithm can be used to find the maximal regions of the active surface. While this method sounds simple, the cost of this computation is excessive. Faster methods are possible by rearranging the order of calculations.

There is no need to recalculate all possible active surface regions for each point on the surface. By keeping track of the size of each region and the "largest-region identifier" for each pixel in the image in a buffer, only one pass through the regions is required. This buffer is initialized to contain the identifier of a zero-area region. For each pixel in each possible region, the size of the current region is compared to the size of the region in the buffer. If the current region is larger, the buffer is updated to contain the current region identifier. Thus, the maximal regions can be determined with only one pass through all possible active surface regions. This modified algorithm yields the desired results but is still rather costly to compute because so many regions must be grown.

A good approximation to the "correct" maximal regions can be calculated quickly by using a subset of the active surface points as the seeds for growing regions. The program begins by using every 100th point on the active surface as a seed and calculating the active surface regions associated with these points. If the seed point has already been identified as part of some region, that seed is ignored because a region including that point has already been identified. After one pass through the active surface selecting seeds, many of the maximal regions have been identified. To find the remainder, the program makes a second pass through the surface and uses any point which is not part of some region as a seed point. Once the regions associated with these points are calculated, all of the maximal regions corresponding to the N axis sheets comprising the IAS will be identified. These regions define the IAS partition.

REPRESENTING THE IAS PARTITION

Because the regions in the IAS partition do not overlap, it is possible to represent the IAS partition by recording the region identifier associated with each point on the active surface in a two-dimensional matrix. These values are stored in a grey-scale image using the /usr/image format.

Before the seed selection described above takes place, this image is initialized to contain all zeros (the identifier of a zero area region). The program uses a seed counter to generate unique region identifiers. Thus, after all of the regions have been identified, the output image will contain values from 1 to N corresponding to region identifiers on the active surface. The actual locations of the seeds are not important and are not recorded. This representation of the IAS partition can be input to one of several region analysis or display programs.

DISPLAYING THE IAS PARTITION

Now that the active surface regions associated with the individual IAS sheets have been computed and stored in an image, there are several ways to display this information. The simplest technique is to display the region image generated above. This gives an overall impression of the IAS partition but is difficult to interpret because adjacent regions often have very similar region numbers (see Figure 3.4). Displaying the boundaries between all of the regions in the image gives a better indication of the shape of the region associated with each IAS sheet. These boundaries can be easily calculated by scanning the maximal-region image from top to bottom and left to right and detecting changes in region numbers.

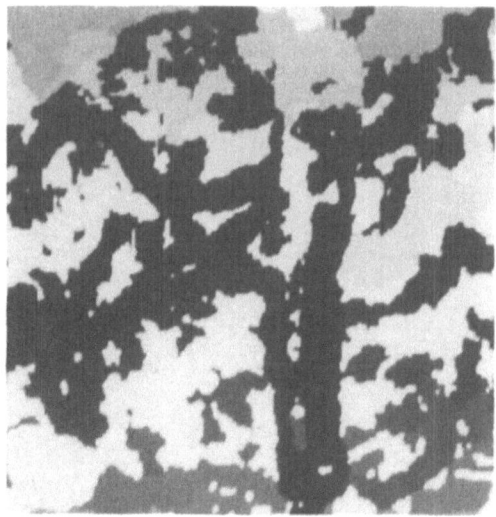

FIGURE 3.4. IAS regions displayed by number for a DSA image.

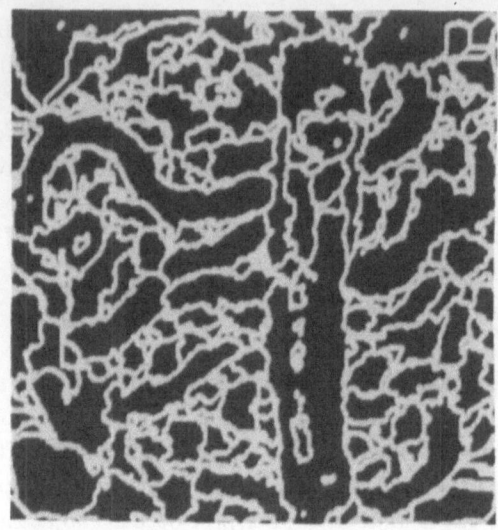

FIGURE 3.5. IAS region boundaries for a DSA image.

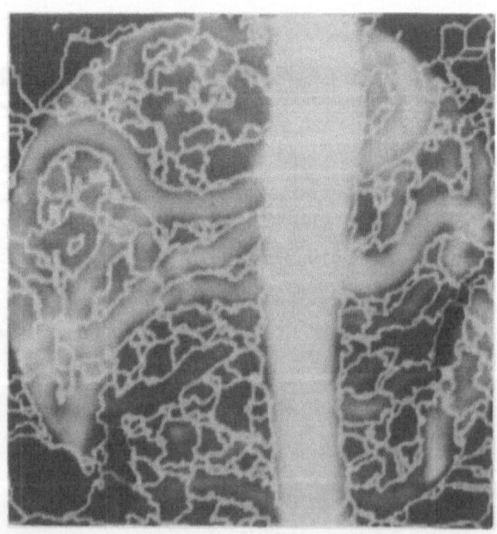

FIGURE 3.6. IAS region boundaries superimposed on a DSA image.

This technique produces satisfactory results (see Figure 3.5). When these boundaries are superimposed on the original grey-scale image, the relationship between image structures and IAS sheet regions can be investigated (see Figure 3.6). Interactive region selection techniques are also possible and are described in detail in the next chapter.

3.2.6. Calculating the Radius and Curvature Functions

Two other IAS properties are useful in the analysis of object shape. We can study the width and bending behavior of structures in the image by examining the radius function and curvature properties of the active surface. While these are the last components of our shape description, they are essential for detailed shape analysis applications.

The radius function gives the width of image structures. In addition, the rate of change of the radius function specifies how the width of the image structure is changing. Calculating the radius value for every point on the active surface involves finding the distance from the axis point to the nearest point on the image surface at the same intensity. This information has already been calculated and stored in the three-dimensional image symmetry function. Thus, to find the radius function for the IAS only involves a table lookup given the (x, y, I) coordinates of each point on the surface. Current applications of the IAS have not required this radius information, so this lookup function has not yet been implemented.

Axis curvature directly gives the degree of object bending. In addition, the derivatives of curvature describe how the object bending changes as we move along the axis sheet. This information can be used to characterize the shape of individual axis sheets or parts of these sheets. There are several ways axis curvature can be calculated. The most convenient method uses the Weingarten map [Thorpe, 1979]. This quadratic form is calculated from the first and second order partial derivatives of the axis surface and provides a concise description of how the surface normal changes as we move along the surface and hence captures the bending behavior of the surface. As a result, the Weingarten map can be used to calculate the surface curvature in any direction on the active surface. In addition, the principal curvature directions and the Gaussian and mean curvatures of the surface can be determined from the algebraic properties of this map. Current applications of the IAS do not make use of this curvature information so it has not yet been computed.

3.3. Discussion

Calculating an accurate approximation of the IAS for a grey-scale image is not an easy task. Early attempts to calculate this shape description by computing the symmetric axis on a level-by-level basis failed because of the difficulty in connecting these SAs from level to level. This connection problem is avoided by computing all of the SAs simultaneously. To accomplish this task, we developed and implemented the active surface model and related programs to generate the image symmetry function, link quench points on the active surface, and grow regions corresponding to the individual axis sheets which comprise the IAS. These programs have been tested on several images and they produce excellent results. Thus, our primary objective of demonstrating a viable implementation of the discrete IAS has been met.

CHAPTER 4

Segmentation via the Intensity Axis of Symmetry

The previous chapter described how the IAS can be calculated for an image. This chapter explains how the IAS can be used to segment an image into sensible image regions. Before this is demonstrated, several methods for displaying the IAS are illustrated. The chapter concludes with an analysis of the effects of preprocessing the image before computing the IAS and its induced image segmentation.

4.1. Displaying the IAS

The IAS is a collection of surfaces in three dimensions with an associated radius and curvature function at each point on these surfaces. To understand this shape description, we need a way to display this information. This requires a combination of computer graphics techniques and standard image display methods. This section describes three methods for displaying the IAS : (1) using grey-scale images, (2) using wire frame models, and (3) using a simple shaded graphics model called the *intensity top view*.

Recall that the (x, y, I) coordinates of points on the active surface are represented as sampled parametric equations and stored in a three-dimensional image in /usr/image format. Hence, the easiest method for

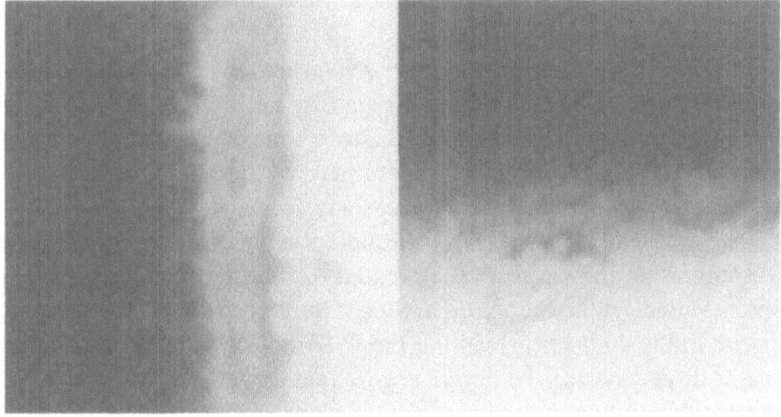

FIGURE 4.1. Grey-scale display of the IAS for a digital subtraction angiogram (DSA) image. The two images represent the x coordinate (left) and the y coordinate (right) of the active surface.

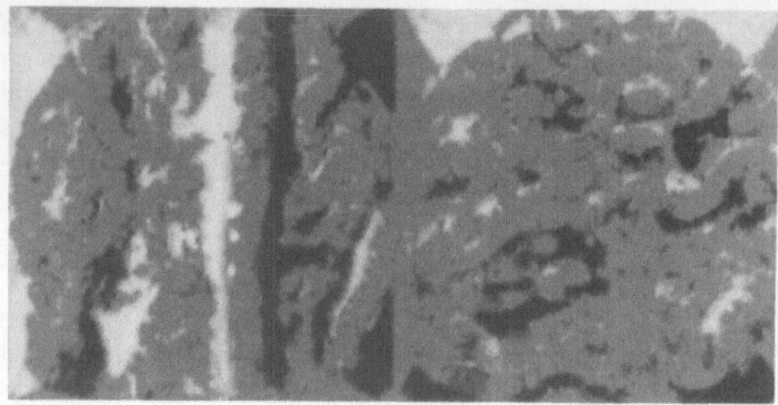

FIGURE 4.2. Change in IAS coordinates displayed as a DSA image. These images represent the change in the x coordinate (left) and the y coordinate (right) of the active surface.

visualizing the IAS is to simply display this grey-scale image. This method is demonstrated in Figure 4.1. Here, the left image gives the x coordinate and the right image the y coordinate of the active surface at each point. Since the active surface is restricted to move only in the spatial dimensions, the intensity coordinate always corresponds to the input image.

The direction of motion and the convergence rate of the active surface can be visualized by subtracting the starting positions of the active surface from the coordinates of the IAS after a selected number of iterations (see Figure 4.2). The intensity coordinate of the active surface never changes, so this part of the difference image will always equal zero.

Because the IAS consists of a collection of surfaces in three dimensions, it is important to understand the spatial relationships among these axis sheets to understand the IAS as a whole. One way to do this is to generate a wire frame model representing the IAS and display this model on a vector display device. To obtain a wire frame representation of the IAS, every Kth point on the active surface is connected in a rectangular mesh, where K is the ratio between the image size and the vector display limit. The global structure of the IAS can be determined by interactively inspecting the resulting wire frame model from different points of view. The relationship between image structures and individual IAS sheets can be

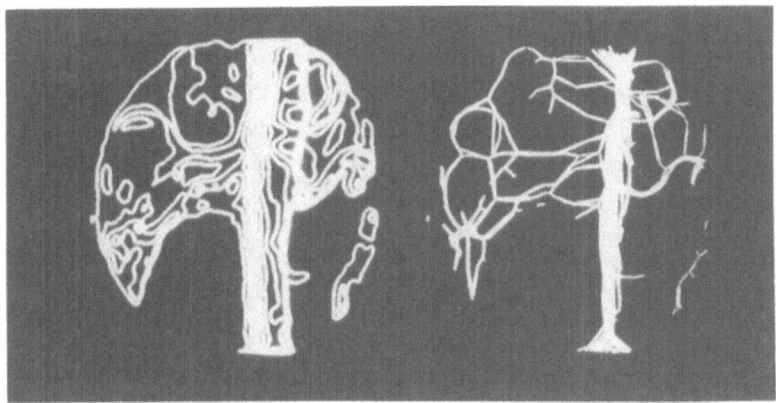

FIGURE 4.3. Wire frame display of a DSA image surface (left) and the surface for the corresponding IAS (right).

understood when the original image surface is also displayed as a wire frame (see Figure 4.3). The wire frame display technique is also helpful for visualizing the convergence of the active surface towards the IAS. Wire frames can be displayed after selected numbers of iterations and compared to see how the active surface is converging under different conditions. The active surface convergence criteria and the partial derivative weights for the active surface functional described in the previous chapter were experimentally determined using this display technique.

The third technique used for visualizing the IAS is based on a simple shaded graphics model. The active surface is represented by a collection of polygons whose vertices are points on the IAS. The color of each of these vertices is equal to the intensity of the active surface at that point. To compare the active surface to the original image, the *top view* of this model is generated. This is accomplished by setting the rendering viewpoint in (x, y, I) to $(0, 0, +\infty)$ and using parallel projection to calculate the visible image. No lighting model is required to capture intensity variation. Instead, the grey level of intermediate points on each polygon is determined using linear interpolation of the intensities of the four vertices. The result is an image which looks like a "thinned" version of the original grey-scale image (see Figure 4.4).

This display technique is useful for illustrating the bending and branching of IAS sheets in the spatial domain and in the intensity domain. The

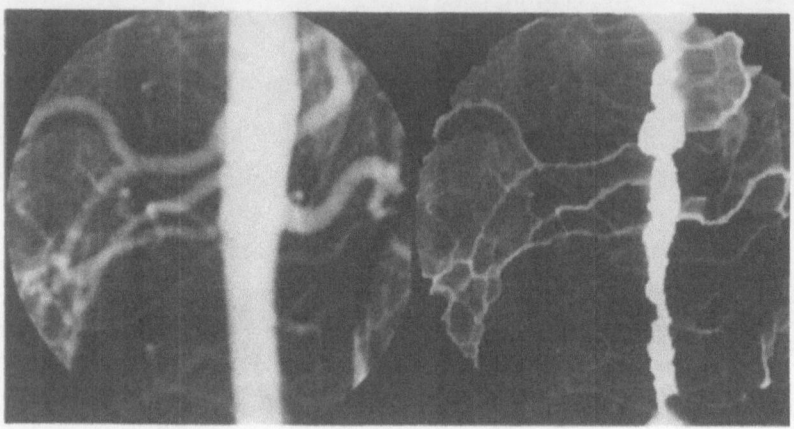

FIGURE 4.4. A DSA image (left) and its corresponding top view of the IAS (right). Notice the central vertical ridge whose width indicates bending of IAS sheets in the intensity dimension.

relatively thin ridges in the top view image are easy to follow and their connections easy to identify visually. Hence, the spatial properties of the IAS can be easily studied. The width of the top view ridges indicates the asymmetry of structures in the original image. Whenever the intensity profile of an intensity ridge is steeper on one side than on the other, the corresponding IAS sheet bends in the intensity dimension. This bending is reflected by wide ridges in the top view image which are brighter on one side than on the other.

4.2. Image Segmentation

Image segmentation is the process of grouping pixels in the image into regions so that each region corresponds to some semantically sensible object. The process of identifying these objects is called labeling. Lifshitz [Lifshitz, 1987] and others have shown that multiresolution analysis can be applied to obtain more successful segmentations than conventional techniques based on local pixel properties or measures of edge strength [Ballard and Brown, 1982]. Following Crowley [Crowley and Parker, 1984], we argue that yet better segmentations can be obtained by using global information provided by image shape analysis. The next section describes how the IAS can be used to segment images into visually sensible regions. The subsequent section describes the results of this segmentation method and discusses several potential applications of image regions identified using this technique.

4.2.1. Segmentation Method

Partitioning an image into visually sensible regions requires some decision algorithm that reflects what we mean by "visually sensible". Since a single axis sheet represents a single geometric structure in the image, generating the image regions "related" to individual IAS sheets will result in regions which reflect the global shape properties represented by the IAS. These regions are likely to describe meaningful structures in the original image.

There are two natural ways to determine the image regions related to individual IAS sheets. The first method for generating the grey-scale region associated with an axis sheet uses the inverse mapping of the IAS described in Chapter 2. Here, the radius function on the axis sheet is used to calculate the volume defined by the union of all maximal disks centered on their respective axis points. The maximal intensity at each (x, y) location of this volume describes a grey-scale image associated with the axis sheet. The problem with this approach is that maximal disks for adjacent IAS sheets overlap. As a consequence, the image regions corresponding to IAS sheets overlap rather than partitioning the image into disjoint segments. This method is rejected for this reason. The second method for relating axis sheets to image regions uses the active surface partition described in Chapter 3. Each region in this partition is comprised of the active surface points which map to a single IAS sheet. Hence, these active surface regions define a disjoint segmentation of the original grey-scale image into visually sensible components. This is illustrated in the next section.

4.2.2. Segmentation Results

To display the active surface regions, we implemented an interactive region display program. This program operates as follows. First, the original grey-scale image is displayed in one portion of the display window. Then, the user selects a point in this image using the mouse. The

(x, y) coordinates of the selected point are used to look up the region identifier for the region containing that point. This region identifier information was pre-calculated and stored in a region image by the IAS partitioning program. The region image is then used as a mask to identify all other image points which lie in the same region. These points are displayed in their original intensities in an adjacent portion of the display window. All points which are not in this region are displayed in black.

The results of this region definition and display method on vascular images are very encouraging. Image regions associated with individual blood vessels are routinely identified in digital subtraction angiogram (DSA) images. This is demonstrated with three different DSA images in Figure 4.5. In each case, most of the major blood vessels and other symmetrical structures in the image are described by single IAS regions. In addition, many smaller blood vessels are identified. This result is particularly significant because image contrast in these regions is low. Large image structures which have superimposed detail are not as easily identified. For example, several image regions are required to construct the central vertical vessel in Figure 4.5. This is because the IAS sheet associated with this structure has several smaller sub-sheets attached to it which act as boundaries in the region growing algorithm described in Chapter 3. With some means for identifying this relationship between IAS sheets, the single image region associated with an axis and its sub-axes could be automatically displayed. These relationships between axis sheets can be specified manually using a hierarchy editor [Coggins, 1988], or automatically by exploiting multiresolution properties of the IAS. The second alternative is discussed in detail in the next chapter.

The results of this segmentation technique on other types of medical images are mixed. Bones and other elongated anatomic structures can be easily selected in computed tomogram (CT) images and dental radiographs, but non-symmetrical or blob-like structures are not as easily identified. In certain cases, image structures which are described by multiple IAS sheets are composed of several image regions. For example, the left kidney in the CT image in Figure 4.6 is composed of two IAS regions. This is not a problem; it reflects the desirable decomposition of complex objects into sub-objects. Semantically meaningful image regions can easily be obtained by interactively combining these IAS regions. In other situations, a single IAS region corresponds to several adjacent anatomical structures. For example, the IAS region near the spinal cord in the CT

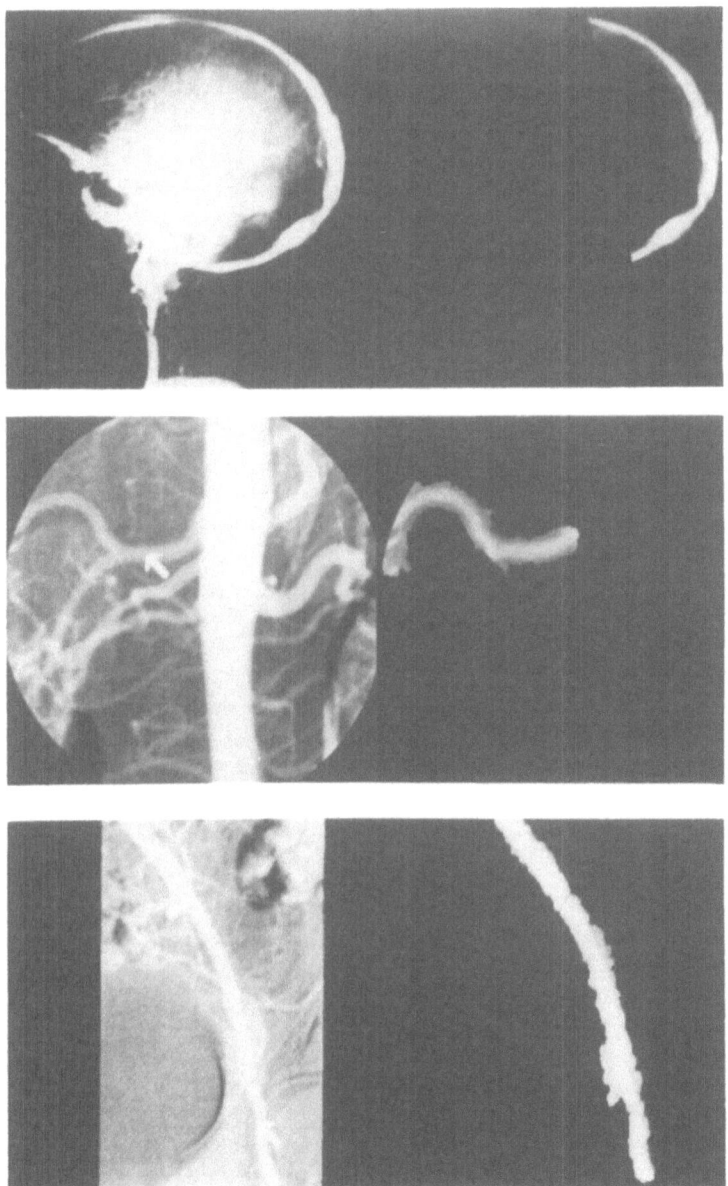

FIGURE 4.5. Three DSA images and corresponding blood vessel regions; a carotid arteriogram (top left and right), a renal arteriogram (center left and right), and a left iliac arteriogram (bottom left and right).

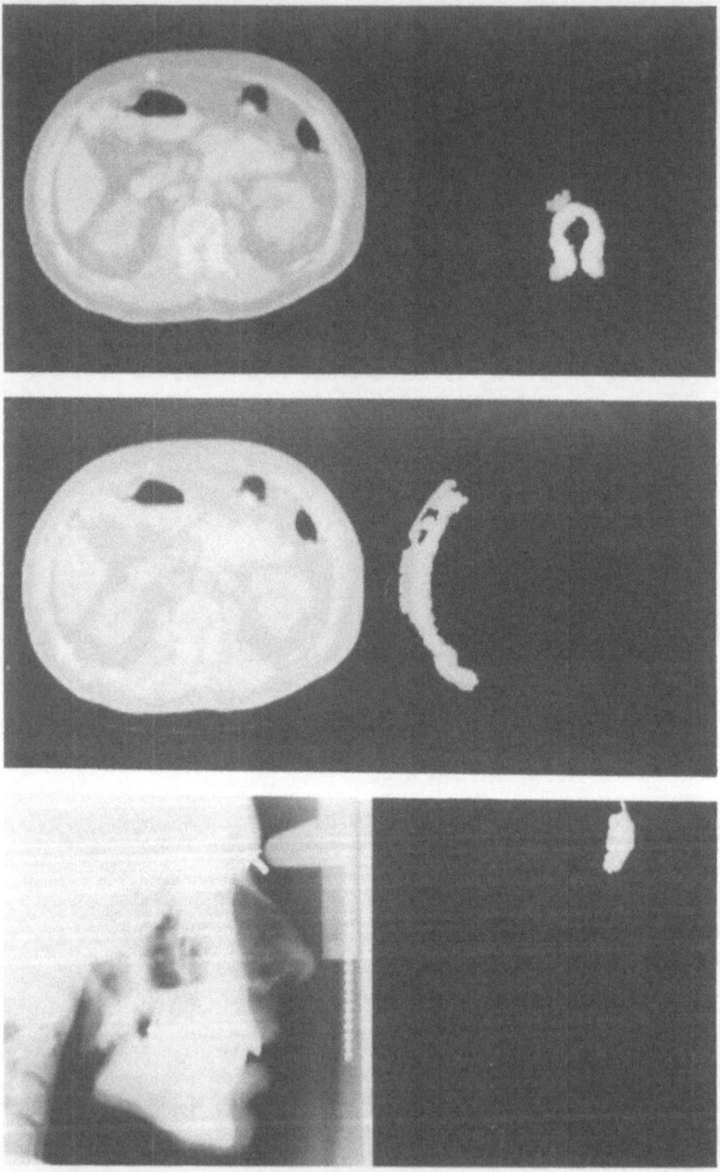

FIGURE 4.6. An abdominal CT image (top and center) and a dental radiograph (bottom) and a collection of anatomical structures associated with individual IAS regions for these images (right).

image in Figure 4.6 also includes adjacent muscle tissue. This is a serious problem. Separate objects should be described by separate IAS structures and correspond to separate IAS image regions. To overcome this difficulty requires some means of manually editing the image regions produced by the IAS to obtain portions of the image corresponding to semantically meaningful regions of interest (ROI) in medical images.

One problem with this segmentation method is that the image regions defined by this scheme are normally wider than expected by human observers. This is because IAS regions are defined to be image structures which are symmetrical about some central axis. Thus, these regions extend from the top of one ridge to the bottoms of adjacent valleys, not merely to the steepest points on the hillsides. Hence, the resulting regions are not bounded by edges. The fact that these image segments include neighboring edges can be useful in some applications. For example, by post-processing selected ROIs to detect edges, it is possible to identify the sub-region bounded by these edges. With these edge-bounded regions, more accurate measurements of anatomical structures can be obtained. By extending ROIs to three dimensions, edge-based volume rendering techniques can be used to visualize three-dimensional anatomical structures, thereby potentially improving image understanding by physicians. Thus, edge information in conjunction with sensible regions of interest defined by the IAS can be very useful in image analysis and display applications.

4.3. Effects of Image Processing

With the tools in place to display the IAS and the image segments associated with individual sheets of the IAS, it is possible to study the effects of image processing on the IAS and on the resulting segmentations. Since the IAS reflects shape properties of the level curves of an image, any image processing which changes the relative intensities of pixels in the image will result in different IAS descriptions than the original image. Three classes of image operations are considered here: methods for improving the contrast in images, methods for smoothing images via blurring, and methods for measuring edge strengths in images. The remainder of this section describes the effects of these operations.

4.3.1. Contrast Enhancement

It is common practice to enhance the contrast of medical images to facilitate diagnosis. The goal of these methods is to make structures within the image more visible to human observers. One way to do this is to allocate display intensities in proportion to the number of pixels at each intensity in the image. This technique is called *histogram equalization* because the cumulative histogram of the image is linearized in the process [Castleman, 1979]. Because the relative ordering of pixel values in the image is unchanged by this procedure, the level curves in the image will remain unchanged. Hence, the IAS of images processed in this way will remain essentially identical to the IAS for the original image. Only the curvature function in the intensity dimension will be affected. As a consequence, the image regions defined via the IAS will remain unchanged if an image histogram is equalized.

More effective contrast enhancement is possible by focusing on more local image properties. By performing a histogram equalization for a given neighborhood around each point in the image, pixels can be displayed with an intensity which reflects their brightness relative to other points within this neighborhood. This contrast enhancement technique is called *adaptive histogram equalization* (AHE) [Pizer, 1987b]. Unlike global histogram equalization, AHE changes the relative ordering of pixels values in the image. Thus, the level curves in the image are changed, causing the IAS for AHE-processed images to differ from the IAS for the original image. For the three DSA images tested, the effect of this change on the resulting segmentation yields mixed results. In some cases it aids the identification of low contrast image structures, while in others it makes the identification of larger image structures more difficult (see Figure 4.7). It appears that this type of local contrast enhancement emphasizes local shape over global shape and these changes are reflected in the structure of the IAS. This observation remains unproven. Further research into the relationship between image shape description and contrast enhancement will yield insights to both processes.

4.3.2. Gaussian Blurring

Whenever image noise is a problem or small image details are not of interest, these structures can be removed from the image by blurring. Numerous smoothing and blurring methods have been devised [Castleman,

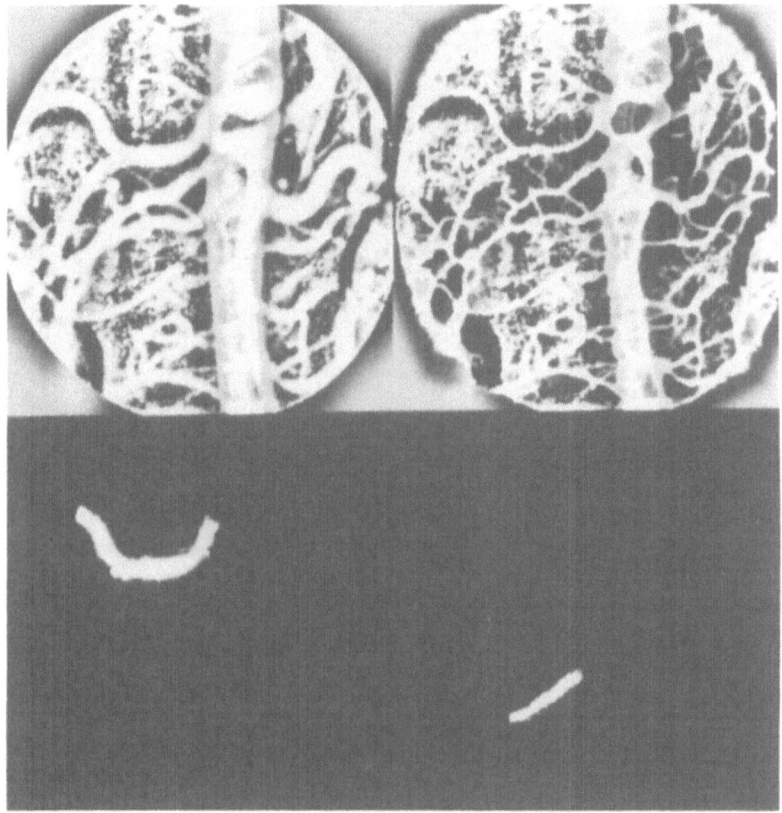

FIGURE 4.7. Effects of contrast enhancement via AHE on a DSA image (top left) and its associated IAS top view (top right) and selected IAS regions (bottom left and right).

1979], but convolution with a Gaussian kernel has the most desirable properties [Koenderink, 1984; Babaud 1986]. Because blurring involves calculating weighted averages of pixels in small neighborhoods, the relative ordering of pixel values in the image will be changed when an image is blurred. Hence, the IAS and corresponding image segmentation for a blurred image will differ from those calculated for the original image. The complexity and number of axis sheets and associated image regions generally decreases as the degree of blurring increases (see Figure 4.8). As a result, Gaussian blurring is useful for multiresolution analysis.

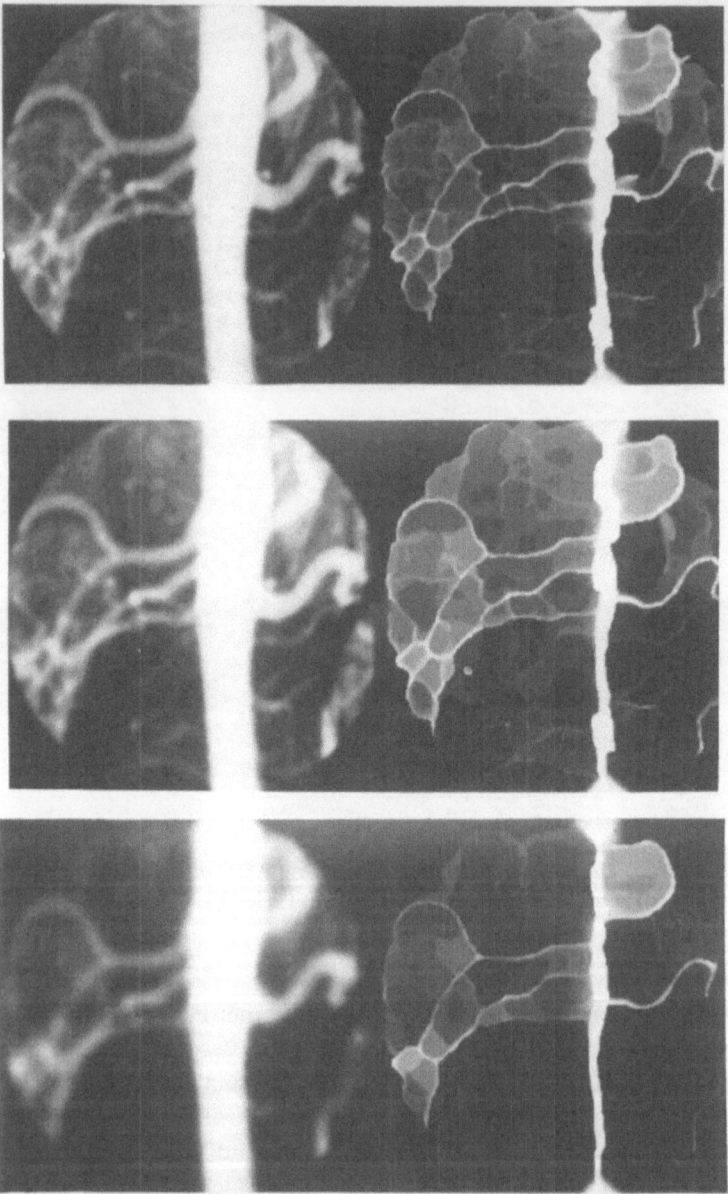

FIGURE 4.8. Effects of blurring a DSA image with a series of Gaussians (left) and their associated IAS top views (right). The standard deviations of the Gaussian filters in the frequency domain are: 30, 20, 10 (from top to bottom, respectively).

The degree of blurring required to annihilate image structures can be used to measure the "importance" of these structures. This approach can be used to obtain the hierarchical relationship between axis sheets and their corresponding image regions. This process is described in Chapter 5.

Before multiresolution analysis can proceed, the original grey-scale image must be preprocessed to handle certain boundary conditions. For an image of infinite extent, blurring with a Gaussian is equivalent to diffusion according to the heat equation and eventually results in an

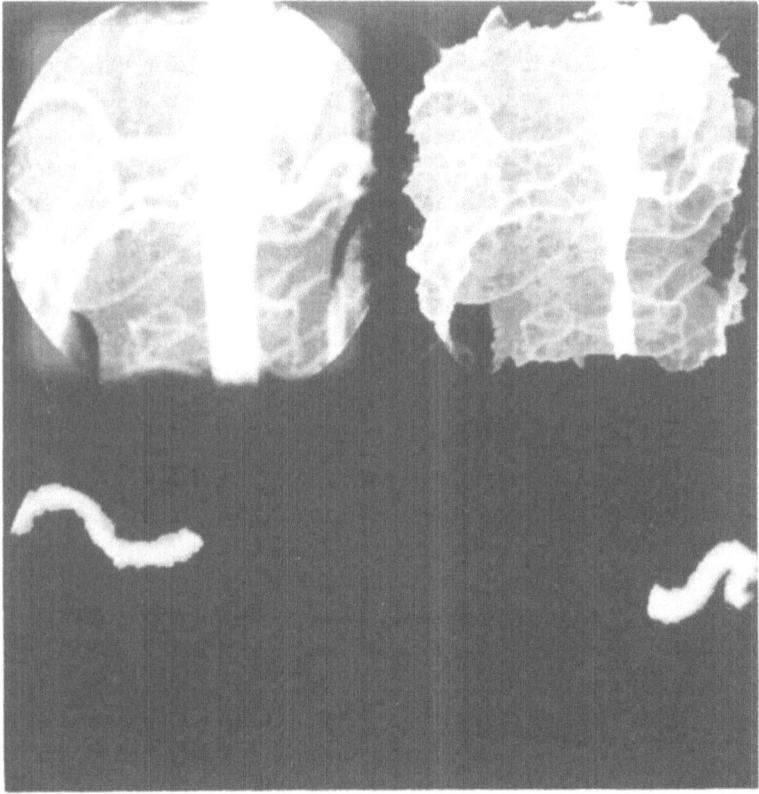

FIGURE 4.9. Effects on the IAS of preprocessing for Gaussian blurring on a DSA image (top left) and associated IAS top view (top right) and selected IAS regions (bottom left and right).

image with only one extremum [Koenderink, 1984]. Typical medical images have finite extent and non-zero boundary pixels. Correctly modeling the diffusion process to avoid edge effects for such images involves four steps:

1. calculating the image which has the same boundary conditions as the original image and is invariant under blurring,
2. subtracting this image from the original image to obtain an image with zero boundary,
3. eliminating image boundaries by treating the image as an infinite periodic function, and
4. using Gaussian blurring on the resulting image to study the multiresolution behavior of the original image [Lifshitz, 1987].

The effects of this preprocessing depend on the distribution of pixel values along the image boundary. For images with few non-zero pixels on the boundary, the blurring-invariant image has little structure. When this image is subtracted from the original grey-scale image, the resulting IAS is only slightly altered near the image boundary. Images with more complex boundary value distributions have more substantial corresponding blurring invariant images. The subtraction of these images from the original has more impact on the IAS and its induced image segmentation (see Figure 4.9). These effects remain to be quantified.

4.3.3. Edge Strength Images

Many computer vision approaches focus on the edges in an image because they provide important information about the structure of objects within images. The IAS reflects image symmetry well, but edge information is captured only indirectly via the derivative properties of the radius function. In an attempt to incorporate edge information more directly, the behavior of the IAS on edge strength images was investigated. Here, the magnitude of the gradient vector is used as an estimation of edge strength at each point in the image. While the relationship between the original image and this edge strength image is visually apparent, the IAS structures for these two images are very different. Each symmetrical object in the original image is represented by a single IAS sheet while the two edges which define the boundaries of this object in the edge strength image will be represented by a pair of IAS sheets (see Figure 4.10).

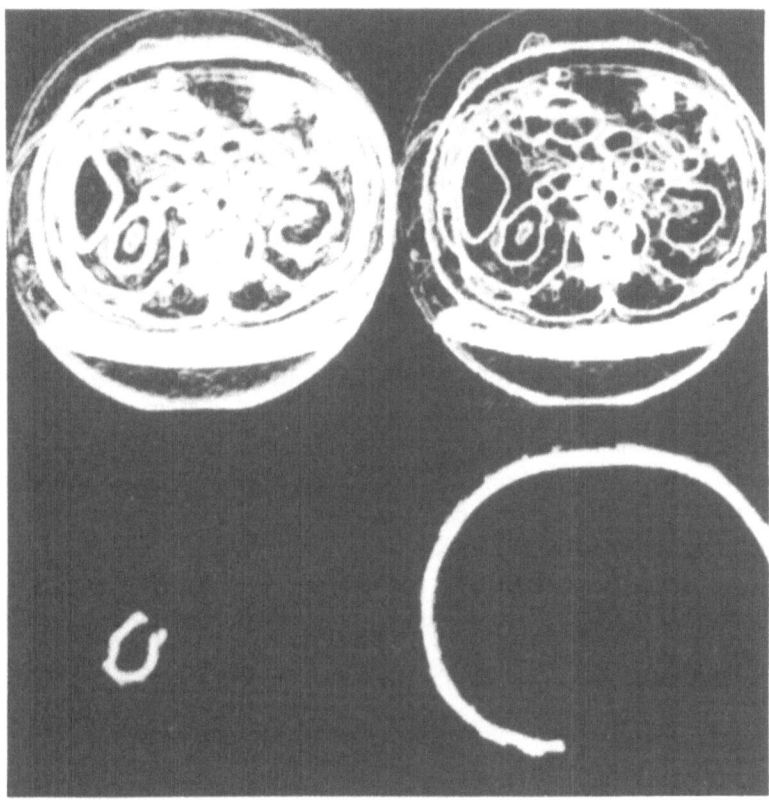

FIGURE 4.10. An edge strength image for a slightly blurred CT image (top left) and its associated IAS top view image (top right) and selected IAS regions (bottom left and right).

Although the edge strength image has a much more complex IAS structure than the original image, the image regions associated with the edge strength IAS are still quite useful. One of the major strengths of IAS-based segmentation is that the resulting image regions are geometrically related. In edge strength images, these regions correspond to connected components of object edges. Since edge following in medical images is often a difficult task, these IAS regions can be used to simplify this process. For example, the boundary of some complex object in an image can be interactively constructed by selecting a collection of edge regions around the perimeter of the object. The "true" location of the object boundary can then be determined using the directional derivative properties of the image gradient [Canny, 1984] within the resulting boundary region. This method for identifying edge locations in images provides useful information to applications which focus primarily on object boundaries and provides another robust way for identifying ROIs in medical images.

4.4. Discussion

The purpose of the IAS is to capture and represent image shape so that applications can use this information for their benefit. To demonstrate that the IAS achieves this goal, we have described how image segmentation is improved by focusing on geometric properties of image structures via the IAS. In addition, the effects of three types of image processing on the IAS and its induced image segmentation have also been investigated. There are many other potential applications of the IAS and many other image processing effects to be studied which are beyond the scope of this research.

CHAPTER 5

Multiresolution Analysis of the Intensity Axis of Symmetry

The previous three chapters defined the intensity axis of symmetry (IAS), described an implementation of the IAS and illustrated the application of this shape description to the problem of image segmentation. This chapter describes the multiresolution behavior of the IAS and outlines two methods for calculating a quasi-hierarchical shape description based on this information. The first method uses the close relationship between symmetry and maximal curvature while the second approach makes use of the approximate relationship between symmetry and watershed boundaries. This chapter concludes with a summary of unsolved problems and suggestions for future work.

5.1. Early Multiresolution Analysis

Most current models of the human visual system recognize that images are simultaneously processed at multiple scales [Ginsburg, 1977; Wilson, 1979; Robson, 1983; Koenderink, 1987]. This multiresolution approach has also been used in computer vision to provide efficient analysis [Burt, 1983; Rosenfeld, 1984b] and also to identify the scale of image structures and to determine the relationships among these structures [Crowley, 1984; Bergholm, 1987]. A particularly promising class of multiresolution methods follows essential image features to annihilation under resolution reduction to determine the scale associated with these structures [Lifshitz, 1987; Gauch and Pizer, 1988]. The fundamental principle used by these methods is that small-scale structures disappear sooner than large-scale structures and that the small image structures annihilate into larger-scale structures. When the relationships between structures can be described by a tree, a scale-based hierarchy on image features can be defined. When more general relationships between structures are possible, like those described by a directed acyclic graph, multiresolution analysis can be used to define a *quasi-hierarchy* which is useful for image segmentation and other computer vision tasks [Coggins, 1988]. This is the case for the IAS, in which loops can appear.

Gaussian blurring is the best choice for resolution reduction because it guarantees image simplification [Koenderink, 1984; Yuille, 1983; Witkin, 1983]. It is the only form of blurring which does not allow the local creation of new values of any linear combination of derivatives of the image as the blurring proceeds. As a consequence, neither image intensities nor Laplacian zeros are created by this process. Nonlinear combinations of derivatives do not share this property. Local intensity extrema (zeros of gradient magnitude) can be created in certain circumstances [Lifshitz, 1987]. This property of Gaussian blurring must be anticipated by computer vision applications which focus on nonlinear derivative properties.

5.2. The Multiresolution IAS

The intensity axis of symmetry captures many aspects of image shape. Unfortunately, as with the symmetric axis, it is too sensitive to noise and small image detail. These minor image features often introduce large but unimportant axis sheets into the IAS. The solution to this problem is to focus on the multiresolution behavior of the IAS to obtain a measure of the importance of each axis sheet. With this information it is possible to define a quasi-hierarchy on the axis sheets which captures this relationship between major and minor image structures. This new data structure can then be used by application programs to direct top-down or bottom-up image analysis tasks.

The obvious method for computing the multiresolution IAS is to blur the input image with a series of Gaussians and compute the corresponding IAS for these images. As noted in Chapter 4, the effect of blurring is

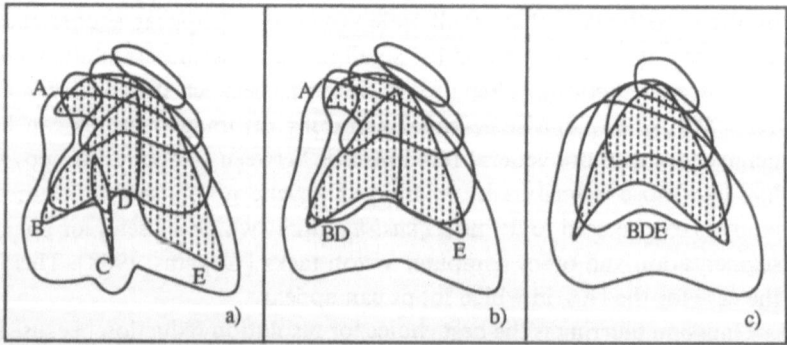

FIGURE 5.1. The IAS quasi-hierarchy induced by image simplification for a synthetic image. Here, branch C annihilates and is identified as a sub-object of the new composite branch BD. Later, branch A annihilates and is identified as a sub-object of the final axis BDE.

to reduce the number and complexity of axis sheets. By selecting the rate of blurring carefully, it should be possible to follow the gradual annihilation of these sheets and define the required axis quasi-hierarchy (see Figure 5.1). This approach was used to calculate the IAS at sixteen selected blurring levels. While the resulting IASs exhibited the predicted behavior, the cost of these computations was excessive.

An alternative approach for computing the multiresolution IAS is to identify an image structure which is directly related to the IAS yet simpler to compute and follow through multiple resolutions. By identifying when components of the simpler structure annihilate, and relating this information back to the IAS, the desired quasi-hierarchy on the IAS can be obtained with less computational expense.

5.3. Multiresolution Vertex Curves

This section describes the theory and implementation issues involved in using curvature information to determine the multiresolution properties of the IAS. The analysis begins with the two-dimensional case, illustrating the relationship between curvature extrema and endpoints of the SA. Then this analysis is extended to the intensity dimension. Curvature extrema of level curves are shown to form connected curves called vertex curves. These curves are directly related to the axis sheets of the IAS, so the multiresolution properties of vertex curves can be used to define the multiresolution IAS. Finally, the difficulties involved in following discrete vertex curves through scale space are discussed.

5.3.1. Boundary Curvature and Vertices

Several researchers have focused on boundary curvature because it reflects the bending of the object, an essential aspect of shape [Brady and Asada, 1984]. Extreme points of boundary curvature (local maxima and minima) can also be used to characterize shapes. If an object boundary is decomposed into sections bounded by two adjacent curvature minima, the resulting boundary segments are called codons [Richards and Hoffman, 1985]. Each codon contains a single curvature maximum and can be characterized into five types depending on the sign of these curvature extrema. By considering sections bounded by adjacent curvature maxima, we get boundary segments called codon duals [Leyton, 1986]. These

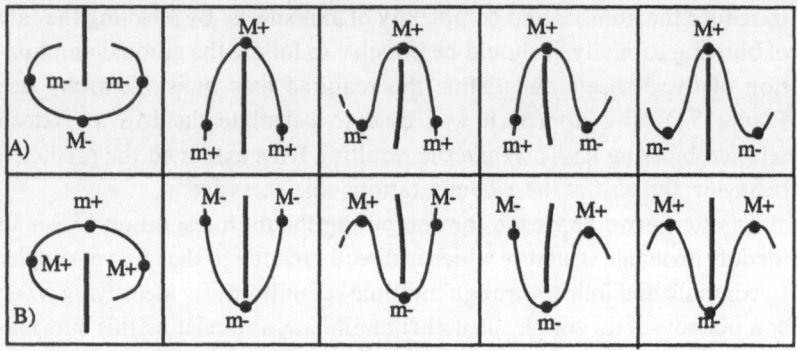

FIGURE 5.2. Relationship between codons and the two-dimensional SA.

can be classified by simply changing the sign and type of each curvature extrema in the codon classification.

Leyton discovered an important relationship between these curvature-based descriptions and the symmetric axis. He proved that each codon has associated with it a unique axis of symmetry and that this line terminates at or near the point of maximal curvature (M) for the codon. Similarly, each codon dual has an associated symmetry line which terminates at a local curvature minimum (m) (see Figure 5.2). The type of SA associated with these boundary segments depends on the type and sign of the curvature extrema. Internal SAs terminate at positive-maxima $(M+)$, external SAs terminate at negative minima $(m-)$, and global SAs are associated with negative maxima $(M-)$ and positive minima $(m+)$. These four types of curvature extrema are also known as *vertices*. Their corresponding points on the SA are called SA *endpoints*. This relationship between vertex points and endpoints of the SA provides a useful tool for studying the SA. Once a boundary has been decomposed into codons (or the vertex points are located), we know the number and location of SA endpoints. This information could be helpful for computing the SA, but it has more important implications for multiresolution techniques.

Under resolution reduction the boundary will tend to simplify. This will cause two adjacent curvature extrema (a local maximum and a local minimum) to move together and annihilate into an inflection point. When this happens, the number of vertex points is decreased by two. The

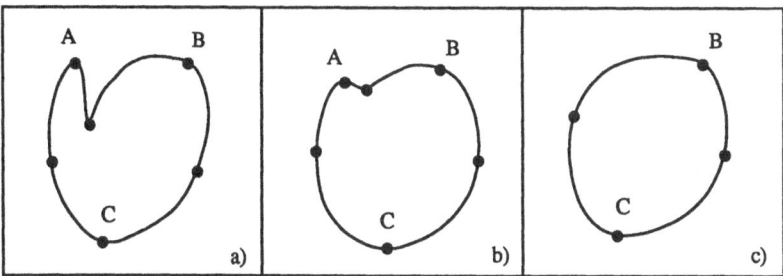

FIGURE 5.3. Multiresolution codon behavior of an object where boundary blurring increases from left to right. Here codon A annihilates into codon B.

problem is to determine which codon annihilated into which. Recall that a codon is a boundary segment bounded by two curvature minima (m) with a curvature maxima (M) somewhere between these points. When two adjacent codons are considered, we have a sequence of five curvature extrema of the form $(m_1, M_2, m_3, M_4, m_5)$, where codon A consists of (m_1, M_2, m_3) and codon B of (m_3, M_4, m_5). We say that codon A annihilates into codon B if M_2 and m_3 are blurred into an inflection point, since two of the three vertex points which comprise codon A have disappeared. Similarly, we say that codon B annihilates into codon A when m_3 and M_4 are blurred together. By recording the level of blurring required to annihilate each codon and also recording which codon blurred into which, it is possible to establish a codon hierarchy (see Figure 5.3).

It has also been demonstrated that in certain circumstances Gaussian blurring imposes a scale-based quasi-hierarchy on the SA branches describing an object [Pizer, 1987]. Because of the correspondence between vertex points and SA endpoints, it is clear that these quasi-hierarchies are related. The scale which causes the annihilation of an axis branch is equal to the annihilation scale for the associated codon and vice versa. This fact can be used to our advantage when computing the multiresolution SA. Vertex points and their associated codons are much easier to compute and follow through scale space than SA branches. Thus, to compute the SA quasi-hierarchy we follow codons through multiple resolutions and use the correspondence between SA endpoints and codons to determine the scale of the individual branches of the SA. This relationship between curvature and symmetry also extends to grey-scale images. Before this can be developed, a review of the differential geometry of surfaces is necessary.

5.3.2. Surface Curvature

Viewing an image as a surface in $\mathfrak{R}^3$, it is possible to use the tools of differential geometry to determine the curvature of curves on this surface. If the surface is given locally by parametric equation $S(u, v) = (S_1(u, v), S_2(u, v), S_3(u, v))$, then it is possible to define the following linearly independent vectors at each point (subscripts u and v denote partial differentiation).

The tangent in the u direction: $\mathbf{S}_u(u, v) = (S_{1u}(u, v), S_{2u}(u, v), S_{3u}(u, v))$.

The tangent in the v direction: $\mathbf{S}_v(u, v) = (S_{1v}(u, v), S_{2v}(u, v), S_{3v}(u, v))$.

The surface normal at (u, v): $\mathbf{N}(u, v) = \mathbf{S}_u(u, v) \times \mathbf{S}_v(u, v)$.

These three vectors are called the *Gauss trihedron*. They form a basis for the space of vectors at each point on the surface and can be used to calculate various surface properties. As with the Frenet frame, it is possible to determine the curvature of curves on a surface in terms of the derivative properties of these basis vectors. This can be accomplished using the directional derivative, in the direction $\mathbf{w}$, of the unit normal vector $\mathbf{N}$

$$D_\mathbf{w}\mathbf{N} = (\mathrm{grad}(N_1) \cdot \mathbf{w}, \mathrm{grad}(N_2) \cdot \mathbf{w}, \mathrm{grad}(N_3) \cdot \mathbf{w}) = \mathbf{w}^t[\mathrm{Jacobian}(\mathbf{N})],$$

where the three components of the normal vector $\mathbf{N}(u, v)$ are $(N_1(u, v), N_2(u, v), N_3(u, v))$. $D_\mathbf{w}\mathbf{N}$ measures the rate of turning of the normal $\mathbf{N}$ as we move on the surface in a direction $\mathbf{w}$. With a change in sign this directional derivative is known in the *Weingarten map*. Because this linear map captures information about the shape of the surface, it is also known in the literature as the *shape operator*. The Weingarten map can be used to calculate the curvature of any curve on the surface S using

$$\kappa(\mathbf{p}, \mathbf{w}) = \boldsymbol{\alpha}''(t) \cdot \mathbf{N}(\mathbf{p}) = -\mathbf{dS}(\mathbf{w}) \cdot D_\mathbf{w}\mathbf{N}(\mathbf{p}),$$

where $\alpha(t)$ is any parameterized curve restricted to the surface S passing through the point $\mathbf{p}$ with velocity $\alpha'(t)$ equal to the surface tangent given by the differential $\mathbf{dS}(\mathbf{w})$ [Thorpe, 1979]. Because this formula gives the component of curvature of the normal in the tangent direction, it is often called the *normal curvature* of the surface. From a computational point of view, normal curvature can be determined using the Jacobian of the normal map as a quadratic form at each point on the surface. When the surface tangents are unit length, this expression for curvature becomes

$$\kappa(\mathbf{p}, \mathbf{w}) = -\mathbf{w}^t [\text{Jacobian}(\mathbf{N}(\mathbf{p}))] \, \mathbf{dS}(\mathbf{w}) \qquad (1)$$

an easy expression to evaluate. It is interesting to note that algebraic properties of the Jacobian of the normal map correspond to geometrical properties of the surface. The eigenvectors of this matrix give the *principal curvature directions* of the surface at that point. These are the directions of maximal and minimal curvature. The eigenvalues of this matrix give the *principal curvatures*, which are the values of the surface curvature in the principal directions. The determinant of this matrix is the product of principal curvatures and is known as the *Gaussian curvature* of the surface. The average of the principal curvature values is known as the *mean curvature* and can be computed via the trace of this matrix. Thus, many important surface properties are accessible once the Weingarten map has been computed.

5.3.3. Level Curve Curvature and Vertex Curves

Recall that the extremal points of boundary curvature are called vertices. The M+ and m− vertices correspond to the SA endpoints in the two-dimensional case. Since we are treating a grey-scale image as a smooth collection of level curves, these vertex points are adjacent from level to level and form continuous curves on the image surface called *vertex curves*. Similarly, connecting SA endpoints from level to level yields curves which mark the top (or bottom) of IAS sheets. These curves are called IAS *end curves*. Extending the relationship between vertex points and SA endpoints, it follows that the M+ and m− vertex curves of an image correspond to IAS end curves. As a result, vertex curves provide a concise description of the branching and bending behavior of structures in the original grey-scale image (see Figure 5.4). The M+ and m− curvature extrema points mark the tops of intensity ridges and bottoms of intensity courses respectively. Because these curves are easier to calculate than the IAS, they can be used to efficiently study the multiresolution behavior of the IAS.

The first step in locating the vertex curves in an image is to derive

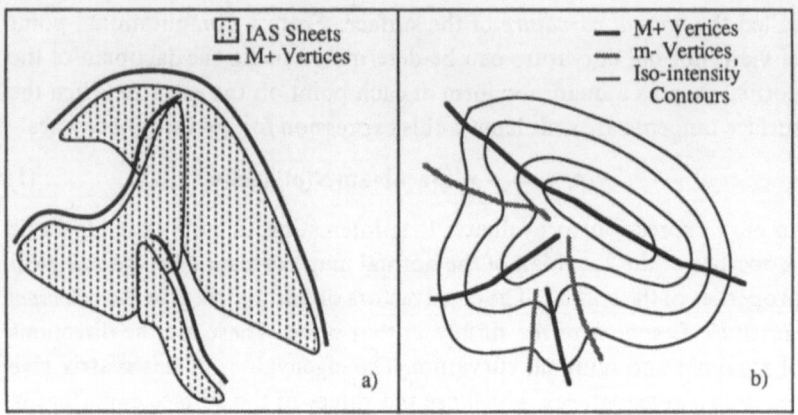

FIGURE 5.4. The relationship between IAS end curves and vertex curves.

an expression for level curve curvature. When an image is represented by the surface $S(u, v) = (u, v, I(u, v))$, the Gauss trihedron reduces to the following:

$$\mathbf{S_u}(u, v) = (1, 0, I_u(u, v)),$$

$$\mathbf{S_v}(u, v) = (0, 1, I_v(u, v)),$$

$$\mathbf{N}(u, v) = (-I_u(u, v), -I_v(u, v), 1).$$

The unit length *level curve normal* is defined by ignoring the third component of the surface normal (which corresponds to the intensity dimension), and scaling the resulting normal so it points inward for closed contours. This yields

$$\mathbf{N}(u, v) = (I_u(u, v), I_v(u, v))/\|(I_u(u, v), I_v(u, v))\|.$$

The unit vector with no intensity component which is orthogonal to the level curve normal is called the *level curve tangent*. This vector is given by

$$\mathbf{T}(u, v) = (-I_v(u, v), I_u(u, v))/\|(I_u(u, v), I_v(u, v))\|.$$

Now we return to the task of calculating the level curve curvature using Equation 1. Since the unnormalized level curve normal in this case equals the image gradient, the Jacobian of the normal map is equal to the

Hessian of the original image. By using the level curve tangent as the surface tangent w, the expression for level curve curvature becomes

$$\kappa(u, v) = -\mathbf{T}(u, v)^t[\text{Hessian(I)}]\mathbf{T}(u, v).$$

This reduces to the following nonlinear combination of first and second partial derivatives of the original image:

$$\kappa(u, v) = -(I_{uu}(I_v)^2 - 2I_{uv}I_uI_v + I_{vv}(I_v)^2)/((I_u)^2 + (I_v)^2)^{3/2}. \tag{2}$$

To evaluate this expression and calculate the level curve curvature at every point in an image requires an estimate of these first and second order partial derivatives. To ensure high quality results, piecewise cubic splines are fit to the image data and the first order partial derivatives of these splines are analytically evaluated and recorded. To estimate the second order partial derivatives of the image, piecewise cubic splines are fit to the first partial derivatives and the first order derivatives of these splines are analytically evaluated. This method can be extended to obtain smooth estimates of higher order partial derivatives. Once the 2-jet is calculated, it is then stored in a three-dimensional image in /usr/image format and later input to the curvature calculation program. The output of this program is a grey-scale image with brightness reflecting the curvature at each image point.

The results for medical images illustrate the relationship between level curve curvature and the structure of the image. Consider the two grey-scale images in Figure 5.5. The image on the left is a digital subtraction angiogram (DSA) image. The image on the right is its corresponding level curve curvature image. Notice how the tops of ridges in the DSA image correspond to bright curves in the curvature image. These bright points are where level curve curvature is maximal and positive. The bottoms of courses in the DSA image have negative minimal curvature and appear as dark curves in the curvature image.

One way to calculate the locations of these curvature extrema is to find the zeros of the directional derivative of level curve curvature

$$D_w\kappa = \text{grad}(K(u, v)) \cdot \mathbf{w},$$

where w is the level curve tangent vector $\mathbf{T}(u, v) = (-I_v(u, v), I_u(u, v))/ \|(I_u(u, v), I_v(u, v))\|$. This expression can be expanded to yield the following nonlinear combination of first, second, and third order partial derivatives of the original image.

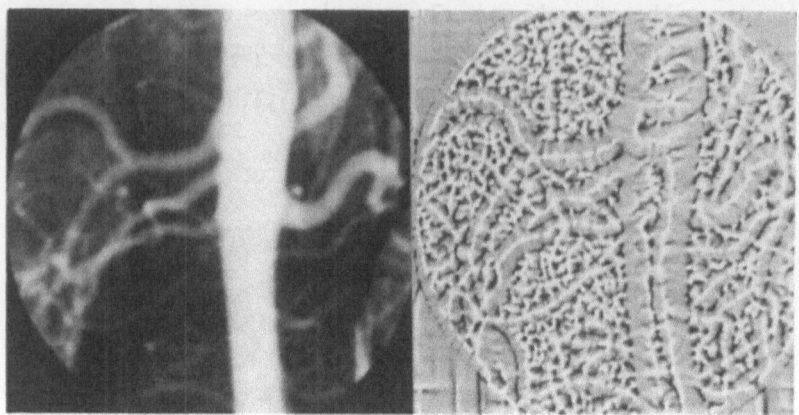

FIGURE 5.5. A DSA image (left) and its corresponding level curve curvature image (right).

$$D_w \kappa = [I_{uuu}((I_u)^2(I_v)^3 + (I_v)^5)$$
$$+ I_{uuv}(-3(I_u)^3(I_v)^2 - 3(I_u)(I_v)^4)$$
$$+ I_{uvv}(3(I_u)^2(I_v)^3 + 3(I_u)^4(I_v))$$
$$+ I_{vvv}((I_u)^3(I_v)^2 + (I_u)^5)$$
$$+ I_{uu}I_{uv}(-3(I_v)^4 + 9(I_u)^2(I_v)^2)$$
$$+ I_{uu}I_{vv}(3(I_u)(I_v)^3 - 3(I_v)^3(I_v))$$
$$+ I_{uv}I_{vv}(3(I_u)^4 - 9(I_u)^2(I_v)^2)$$
$$+ (I_{uu})^2(-3(I_u)(I_v)^3)$$
$$+ (I_{uv})^2(6(I_u)(I_v)^3 - 6(I_u)^3(I_v))$$
$$+ (I_{vv})^2(3(I_u)^3(I_v))]$$
$$/((I_u)^2 + (I_v)^2)^3. \qquad (3)$$

While this is not a pretty expression, it can be evaluated easily, given the 3-jet of the image. Cubic splines are used to calculate these partial derivatives which are then stored in a three-dimensional image in /usr/image format. Using these values, the expression above is evaluated and the results recorded in a real-valued image. The zeros of the curvature

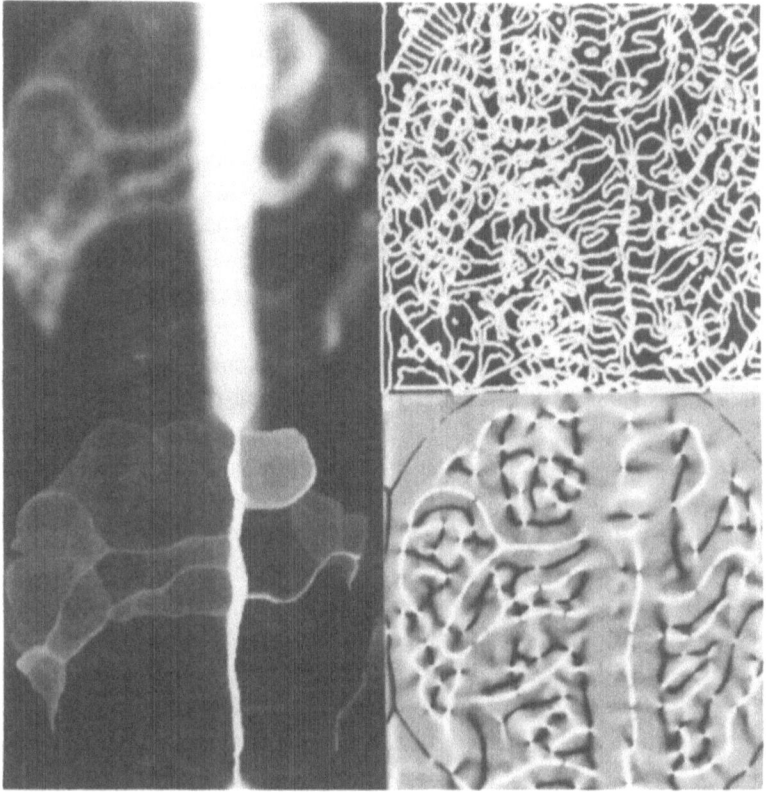

FIGURE 5.6. A blurred DSA image (top left), its corresponding IAS top view image (bottom left), its level curve curvature image (bottom right), and vertex curve image (top right) marking the zeros of the curvature derivative function.

derivative function are located by scanning this image from top to bottom and from left to right to detect sign changes. These pixels are marked as curvature extrema (vertex) points in an output image (see Figure 5.6). Notice that there are more vertex curves in this image than bright or dark curves in the corresponding curvature image. In addition to identifying the vertex curves corresponding to IAS sheets, the zeros of the curvature derivative also identify curves of negative curvature maxima and positive curvature minima. These curves do not correspond to IAS sheets.

5.3.4. Vertex Curve Topology

Before the multiresolution properties of vertex curves can be investigated, the topological structure of vertex curves must be discussed. When a surface $(u, v, I(u, v))$ is smooth and continuous, the level curves defined by $I(u, v) = C$ will also be smooth. It follows that the curvature of these curves will also vary smoothly along the curves and that the points of local maximum and minimum curvature on these curves are connected from level to level and form the vertex curves described above. The exception is at critical points of the image where two or more vertex curves cross.

At local intensity extrema the topology of level curves changes. Slightly below a local intensity maximum the level curve is generally elliptical. Thus, it contains four curvature extrema, two maxima and two minima. As we move towards the critical point, the level curves shrink and these four vertices approach each other. At the local maximum, the level curve reduces to a point and the four vertex curves defined by these points meet. Similarly, four vertex curves meet at each intensity minimum in the image (see Figure 5.7).

At saddle points, the topology of the level curves also changes with intensity. The level curves at the saddle intensity cross while the level curves slightly above and below each saddle are generally hyperbolic near the critical point. Thus, we have a point of locally maximal curva-

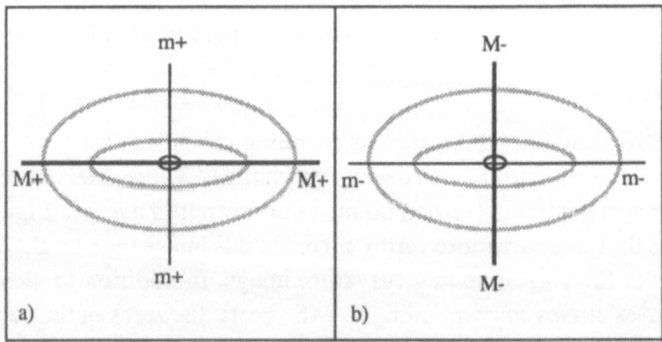

FIGURE 5.7. Vertex curve behavior near an intensity maximum (left) and an intensity minimum (right). Level curves are dotted while vertex curves are solid.

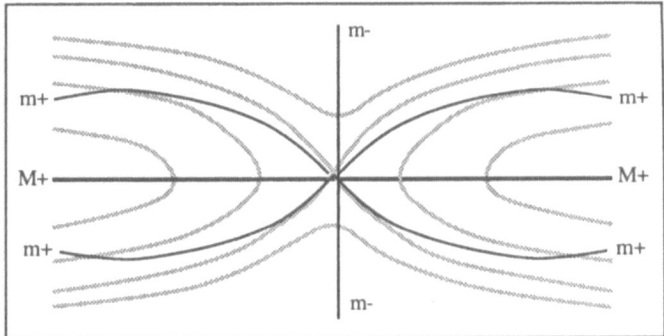

FIGURE 5.8. Vertex curve behavior near an intensity saddle point. Level curves are dotted while vertex curves are solid.

ture on each level curve above these critical points, and a point of locally minimal curvature on each level curve below. Farther away from the critical point, the level curves pull away from the asymptotic directions of the hyperbola. This introduces four points of locally minimal curvature which are also above the critical point. These minima are located on either side the curvature maxima for these level curves. This collection of eight vertex points smoothly approach each other and meet at the saddle point (see Figure 5.8). While Nackman identified three types of saddles in his analysis of critical point configuration graphs [Nackman, 1984], all three exhibit the behavior described above within a small neighborhood of the saddle point.

Finally, the *catastrophe points* of level curve curvature must be considered. Examining the level curves slightly above and below such points, we find that curvature along these level curves is given locally by

$$\kappa(s) = s^3 + ts,$$

where s is arc length and t varies with intensity and goes through zero at the catastrophe point. Thus, the level curve on one side of the catastrophe point has two curvature extrema (one maximum and one minimum) while the level curve on the other side has none. As we move towards the intensity of this critical point, these two curvature extrema come together and annihilate at the catastrophe point. Thus, two vertex curves meet at each level curve catastrophe point on the image surface (see Figure 5.9). Those vertex curves consisting of positive curvature maxima (M+) mark

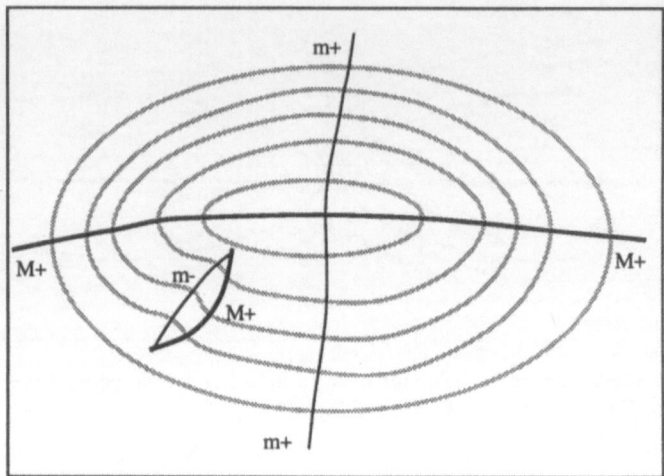

FIGURE 5.9. Vertex curve behavior near two catastrophe points of level curve curvature on a hillside. Level curves are dotted while vertex curves are solid.

the tops of ridges while vertex curves consisting of negative curvature minima (m−) mark the bottoms of valleys in the image.

5.3.5. Multiresolution Properties of Vertex Curves

The effects of Gaussian blurring on critical points in an image are well known [Koenderink, 1984; Lifshitz, 1987]. In general, intensity extrema (maxima or minima) gradually move towards saddle points and annihilate. Occasionally the reverse occurs; an extremum and a saddle point appear from nowhere as the image is blurred. Similar multiresolution behavior has been observed for pairs of curvature catastrophe points. In general, these points move together and annihilate as an image is blurred, but occasionally pairs of curvature catastrophe points are created as the resolution is reduced. How this image simplification process affects vertex curves is more complex. Since all vertex curve segments are bounded at each end by one of the critical points or catastrophe points described above, the annihilation (or creation) of critical points or catastrophe points signals the annihilation (or creation) of vertex curve segments.

The first case to consider is the annihilation of an extremum and a saddle point. As these two critical points come close together, they are connected by three vertex curve segments, one curve corresponding to positive maximal curvature (M+) and two curve segments corresponding to positive minimal curvature (m+). When these points eventually annihilate, these three vertex curve segments annihilate also. At the same time, three pairs of vertex curve segments merge to leave only three vertex curve segments near the annihilation point (see Figure 5.10). The scale of each of the annihilated vertex curve segments is the level of blurring required to cause their annihilation.

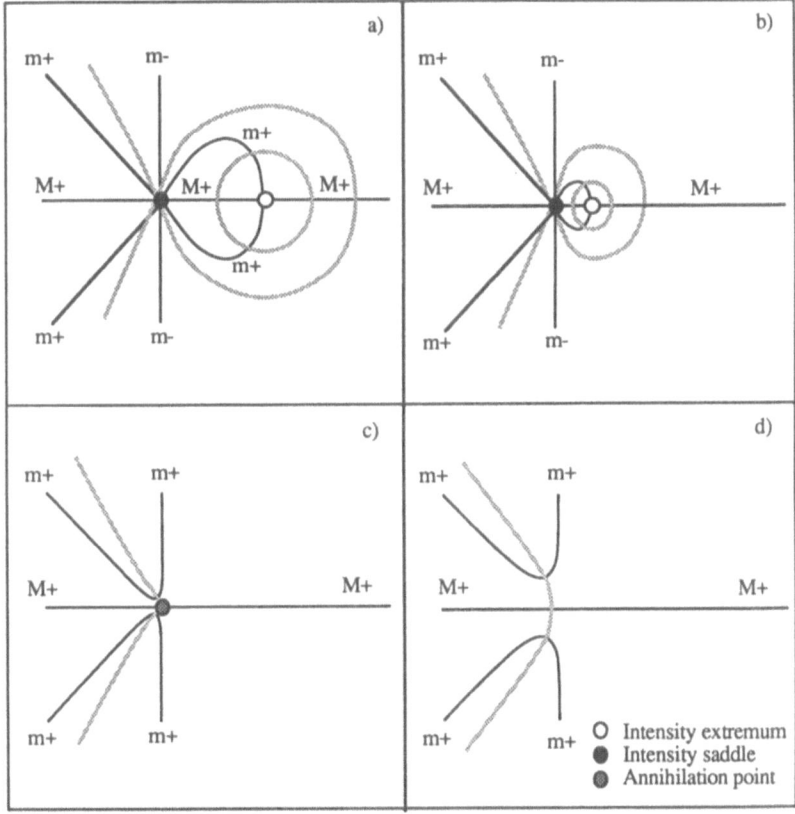

FIGURE 5.10. Annihilation of an intensity extremum and a saddle point as blurring proceeds from frame a) to frame d). Here, level curves of the image are shown dotted while vertex curves are solid.

The next case to consider is the annihilation of pairs of curvature catastrophe points. In the case of a ridge on a hillside, nearby pairs of catastrophe points are connected by a pair of vertex curves, one with positive maximal curvature (M+) and the other with positive minimal curvature (m+). When the image is blurred, these two catastrophe points come together and annihilate. The two vertex curve segments connecting these points are also annihilated (see Figure 5.11). The case where a valley annihilates into the side of a pit is identical except that the signs of the curvature extrema which make up the two vertex curves are negative

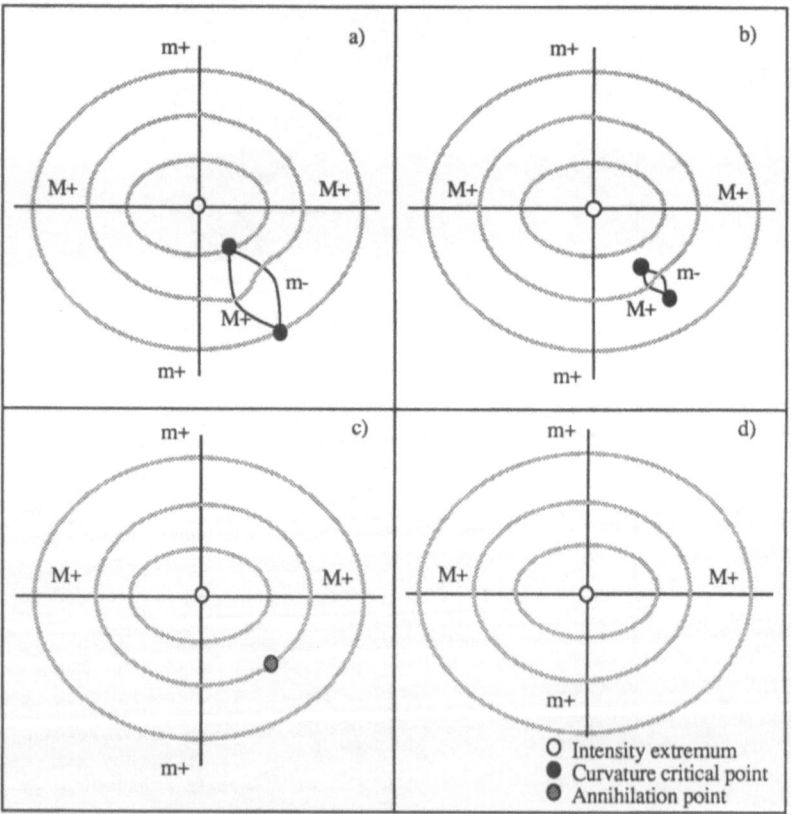

FIGURE 5.11. Simple annihilation of two curvature catastrophe points as blurring proceeds from frame a) to frame d). Here, level curves of the image are shown dotted while vertex curves are solid.

(M − and m −). Again, the scale of each of these vertex curve segments is given by the level of blurring required to cause its annihilation.

The final case to consider involves the temporary creation of a non-generic curvature catastrophe point followed by the annihilation of two curvature catastrophe points which are connected by a single vertex curve segment. Occasionally, curvature catastrophe points move towards other vertex curves as blurring proceeds. Whenever one of these catastrophe points becomes coincident with an existing vertex curve, level curve curvature is given locally by

$$\kappa(s) = s^4 + ts^2,$$

where s is arc length and t varies with intensity and goes through zero at the catastrophe point. Hence, there will be three curvature extrema on one side of this point and one curvature extremum on the other side. As blurring proceeds, this catastrophe point will move away from the vertex curve and become generic again. When this happens, it will then be connected by one vertex curve segment to another catastrophe point and by another vertex curve segment to a critical point in the image. This changes the topology of the vertex curves in this neighborhood (see Figure 5.12). Further blurring in this case will cause the two catastrophe points connected by a single vertex curve segment to come together and annihilate. The scale of this annihilated vertex curve segment is taken as the level of blurring required to cause its annihilation. This also causes the pair of adjacent vertex curve segments to merge, reducing the total number of vertex curve segments in this neighborhood by two.

As noted above, intensity extrema and saddles can be created by Gaussian blurring. In addition, it is possible for pairs of curvature catastrophe points to be created as blurring proceeds. Hence, it is possible for vertex curve segments to be created as resolution is reduced by reversing the three processes described above. While these are not common events, they should be anticipated when studying the multiresolution behavior of vertex curves.

With the theoretical properties of vertex curves in mind, it should now be possible to implement methods to calculate multiresolution vertex curves and use this information to determine the multiresolution properties of the IAS. The first task of calculating vertex curves at multiple resolutions has been solved. This involves evaluating first, second and third order partial derivatives of the image at multiple resolutions and

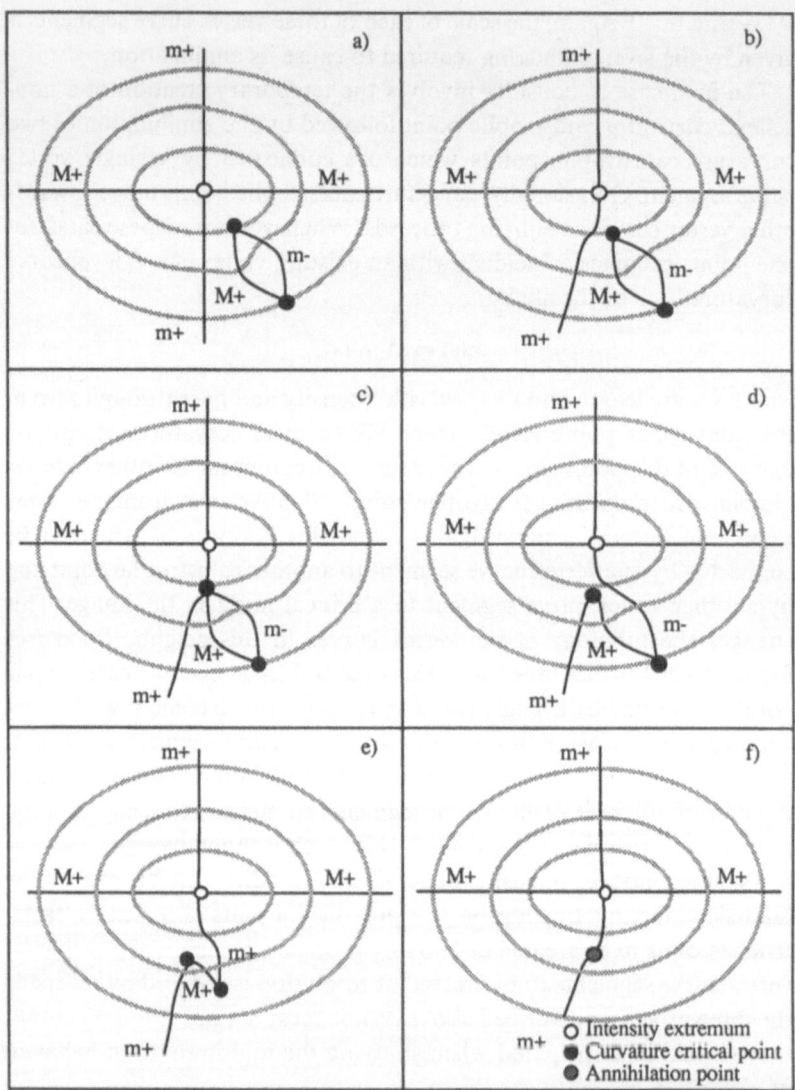

FIGURE 5.12. Complex annihilation of two curvature catastrophe points as blurring proceeds from frame a) to frame f). Here, level curves of the image are shown dotted while vertex curves are solid.

substituting these values into Equation 3 to locate vertex curves at these respective resolutions. To find the multiresolution image sequence, the original image is Fourier transformed and filtered with various Gaussians. To evaluate the partial derivatives of these blurred images, a cubic spline fitting program is used. The results of this sequence of computations verify the theory described above. Vertex curves move smoothly to annihilation, with occasional changes in topology, as blurring level increases (see Figure 5.13).

FIGURE 5.13. Multiresolution vertex curves for a sequence of 16 blurred images (displayed in a 4 × 4 grid). The amount of blurring decreases from left to right and from top to bottom.

The task of identifying individual vertex curve segments and following these segments through blurring has not been solved. The same types of problems encountered in trying to link individual SAs from intensity level to intensity level appear again. The vertex curves calculated above are given only by a collection of pixel locations in an image and are calculated for a finite number of blurring levels. To associate scale with vertex curve segments, these curves must be linked across pixels and from one blurring level to the next. There are three major problems which complicate this task.

First, representing vertex curves as points in digital images introduces pixel artifacts. This is particularly bad near intensity critical points where several vertex curves meet. Thus, the connectivity of vertex curves is difficult to determine. Since much of the analysis of multiresolution behavior of images depends on which vertex curve is connected to which and how these connections change as the image is blurred, these pixel artifacts are a real a problem.

Second, numerical errors in estimating image derivatives affect the quality of curvature calculations. To identify the locations of vertex curves, the zeros of Equation 3 must be calculated. Because this expression involves third order derivatives, and higher derivatives have higher relative error, the derivative of curvature will be less accurate than the value for level curve curvature. Fortunately, this causes only minor problems, especially as blurring proceeds [van Dam, 1988], and the pixel locations of vertex curves remain fairly accurate. To classify the type of curvature extremum on each vertex curve requires the second directional derivative of curvature. Because this function involves fourth order derivatives, there is considerable error introduced when calculating this function. This makes the process of labeling the four types of vertex curves very error prone. Unfortunately, this information is very important for identifying individual vertex curve segments.

Third, vertex curve topology changes as the image is blurred. While level curves change topology from one intensity level to the next near critical points, the overall image can still be represented by a single surface in three dimensions. Thus, the active surface model can be used to maintain coherence across intensities as the IAS is calculated. In contrast, the topology changes in vertex curves from one level of scale to the next are such that the collection can not be represented in scale space by a single surface. Rather, a collection of branching surfaces is required.

The connectivity of these surfaces is quite complex and can not be determined in advance. Thus, efforts to link vertex curves for all levels of blurring simultaneously using an active surface model are hindered by the many changes in vertex curve topology which occur as the image is blurred.

To overcome these difficulties, some means of computing the vertex curves and their connections across blurring levels as a whole is necessary. Until this is accomplished, multiresolution vertex curves can not be used to derive the multiresolution IAS.

5.4. Multiresolution Watershed Boundaries

Focusing on the multiresolution behavior of an even simpler geometric structure, the watershed, avoids the problems described in the previous section. In geography, watersheds are defined in terms of the drainage patterns of rainfall. Regions of terrain which drain to the same point are defined to be part of the same watershed. The same analysis can be applied to images by viewing intensity as height. In this case, the image gradient is used to predict the direction of drainage in an image. By following the image gradient downhill from each point in the image, the set of points which drain to each local intensity minimum can be identified. These are called the *watersheds* of the image. Similarly, the gradients can be followed uphill to local intensity maximum in the image, defining the *watershed duals* of the image. The remainder of this discussion will focus on watersheds, but extends to watershed duals by substituting "up" for "down" and "maximum" for "minimum."

Because watershed boundaries tend to mark the tops of intensity ridges in an image, they tend to approximately coincide with the vertex curves marking the tops of IAS sheets. Hence, one way to approximate the multiresolution behavior of vertex curves and their associated IAS sheets is to focus on the multiresolution properties of watershed boundaries. Since the hierarchy on watershed regions is determined by the multiresolution behavior of intensity extrema in the image, it is easy to calculate the scale of the individual curves which comprise of the watershed boundary and the quasi-hierarchy relating these curves. By relating this information back to the IAS, it is possible to estimate the scale of individual IAS sheets and impose a quasi-hierarchy on these sheets.

The four steps in this process are:

1. calculating the watershed regions and their boundaries for an image,
2. imposing a hierarchy on these regions by following the intensity extrema defining each watershed through multiple resolutions,
3. using the watershed hierarchy to associate an annihilation scale with each watershed boundary curve segment, and
4. relating this watershed boundary information back to the IAS to define a scale-based quasi-hierarchy on axis sheets.

The remainder of this section describes these steps in detail.

5.4.1. Watersheds and Their Boundaries

The first step in calculating the watersheds for an image is identifying the local intensity minima which define the bottoms of watersheds. Since an integer-valued image is a poor approximation to a smooth surface, the input image is converted to floating point and very slightly blurred. This eliminates the plateaus in the image and simplifies the process of identifying maxima and minima. To distinguish between these critical points, each pixel is compared with its eight neighbors. If all neighbors are less than the central pixel, it is identified as an intensity maximum. Similarly, all eight neighbors of an intensity minimum are greater than the central pixel. Once the critical points are identified in an image, their locations are recorded for other programs to use.

The next step is calculating the image gradient. Again, the blurred floating point image is used. Since the goal here is to identify the drainage directions for each pixel in the image, the eight neighbors of each point are searched to determine the maximal and minimal intensity directions. Since there are nine possibilities for each of these directions (the central pixel could also be an extremum), this information is encoded in a single integer value which is then recorded in a grey-scale image.

Partitioning the input image into watersheds begins by marking the locations of intensity minima with unique region identifiers in an output image. Then, for each of the remaining points in the image, the gradient information is used to follow the image down to some intensity minimum. The identifier of this extremum is then recorded in the output pixel corresponding to this starting point. To save computation time, all of the other points along this gradient descent path are also labeled with the same intensity minimum. Once all pixels in the image have been asso-

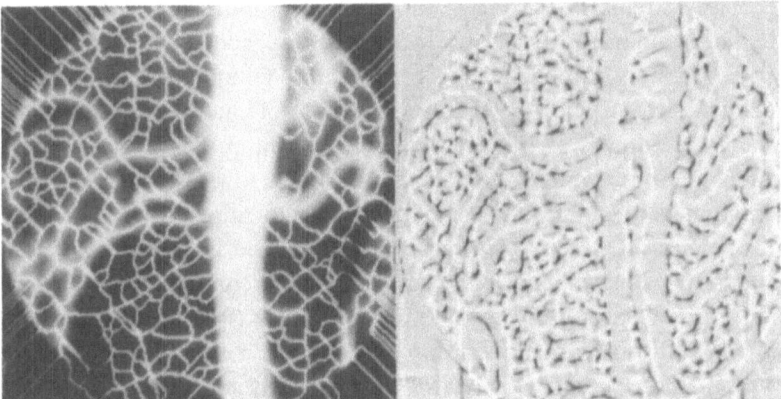

FIGURE 5.14. Watershed boundaries superimposed on a DSA image (left) and vertex curves superimposed on the same image (right).

ciated with their respective minima, the output image will contain the watershed regions of the image. The regions for watershed duals can be calculated using a similar algorithm starting with the intensity maxima in the image and following the image uphill.

The final step of locating the watershed boundaries is accomplished by scanning the region image from left to right and then from top to bottom, detecting changes in region numbers. These locations are then recorded in an output image. Displaying these boundaries superimposed on the original grey-scale image demonstrates the success of this approach for calculating watersheds and also the visual similarity between watershed boundaries and vertex curves (see Figure 5.14). While the correspondence between vertex curves and watershed boundaries is not exact, their visual similarity is often retained as the input image is blurred.

Hence, simple heuristics can frequently be employed to use multiresolution watershed boundaries to obtain a good indication of multiresolution vertex curve and multiresolution IAS behavior.

5.4.2. Linking Intensity Extrema

The multiresolution properties of watershed boundaries depend on the multiresolution behavior of the intensity extrema which define these regions. As an image is gradually blurred with a series of Gaussians, the image structure simplifies. As this blurring progresses, all but one of the intensity extrema in the image will eventually move towards a saddle point and annihilate. The watershed regions associated with these intensity extrema are annihilated at the same time. To impose a multiresolution hierarchy on watershed regions, the paths of intensity extrema in the image are followed as blurring proceeds. When an intensity minimum annihilates into a saddle, the water which drains towards the annihilated minimum will now drain to some other intensity minimum in the image. This defines the parent-child relationship between these two watershed regions. By continuing this process for all extrema in the image, the hierarchy on watershed regions is defined. This task is accomplished by our LINK_EXTREMA program.

Given the original locations of intensity extrema in the image, the extremum linking program operates by following these points through successive levels of blurring. Rather than using the correct but computationally expensive process of linking all image points to their isointensity counterparts from one level of blurring [Lifshitz, 1987], a fast heuristic is employed. Gradient descent is used to link minima from one blurring level to the next. Given an intensity minimum at position (x, y) at blurring level n, the program follows the image gradient downhill from position (x, y) in level $n + 1$ until another intensity minimum is encountered. This is recorded as the link from level n to level $n + 1$ of the former minimum.

The links defined by this process will have duplicates whenever there are fewer extrema in level $n + 1$ than in level n. This occurs whenever local intensity extrema are annihilated. For example, if the extremum at position (x, y) annihilates at blurring level $n + 1$, the extremum at (x, y) will be linked by gradient following to some other pixel at location (x', y') in level $n + 1$. At the same time, a second pixel very near (x', y') in level n will also be linked to (x', y') in level $n + 1$. To determine which link corresponds to the annihilated extremum, the lengths of all links from level to level are compared. If two or more extremum points link to the same point, the extremum with the shortest distance link is selected as the normal link, while the other links are recorded as annihilation links. Thus, each annihilated intensity extremum is linked to the extremum at the next blurring level which is directly downhill from the annihilated extremum. These links between intensity extrema define the hierarchy on their corresponding watershed regions (described above) since gradient descent simulates the effect of water draining on the image surface. The blurring levels required to cause these annihilations are also recorded with these links as an indication of the scale of the watershed regions. This information is used later to identify the scale of individual watershed boundary segments.

This algorithm is less sensitive to the choice of blurring rate than other multiresolution methods because only the intensity extrema in the image are linked from level to level. For this reason, a collection of 50 blurring levels which yield satisfactory results was empirically selected and recorded in a data file used by our LINK_EXTREMA program. Undoubtedly, the blurring rate should be based on properties of the input image. This topic is investigated in detail in Lifshitz's dissertation [Lifshitz, 1987]. Since our current method yields satisfactory results, we have not investigated these options.

5.4.3. Displaying Watershed Region Hierarchies

To examine individual watershed regions, the interactive region display program described in Chapter 4 can be used. Recall that the inputs of this program are (1) the grey-scale image to be displayed and (2) the region image, which acts as a display mask. Thus, the portion of the original image associated with each watershed can be interactively selected and displayed. The resulting image regions are very satisfactory but this technique does not reflect the region hierarchy calculated above.

To visualize this hierarchy on watershed regions, an interactive hierarchy display program was implemented on a color workstation. This program operates as follows. The original grey-scale image is first displayed in one portion of the display window. The user then interactively selects a point in this image using the mouse. The (x, y) coordinates of this point are then used to look up the watershed region which includes that point. This region identifier together with the region image provides a mask for displaying pixels in the adjacent portion of the display window. Points in the same region are displayed in their original grey-scale intensities while the others are left black.

To display the hierarchical relationships among regions, the watershed hierarchy data file calculated by LINK_EXTREMA is read and used to create a table representing the scale at which each region blurs into each other region. There is one row and one column in this table for each of the watershed regions identified in the image. The (i, j)th entry of this table contains the blurring level required for region i to eventually annihilate into region j. In addition to storing the simple links recorded in the hierarchy data file, the non-reflexive transitive closure of these links is calculated and stored. Thus if region A blurs into region B at scale 3, and region B blurs into region C at scale 7, the (A, C)th entry of this table will indicate that A eventually blurs into C at blurring level 7. Cases where region i never annihilates into region j are indicated by -1 in this table.

To display the parent region of the selected region, the user clicks the "increase scale" button on the mouse. The appropriate entry of the hierarchy data file is read to identify which region the selected region annihilated into and the blurring level required to cause this annihilation.

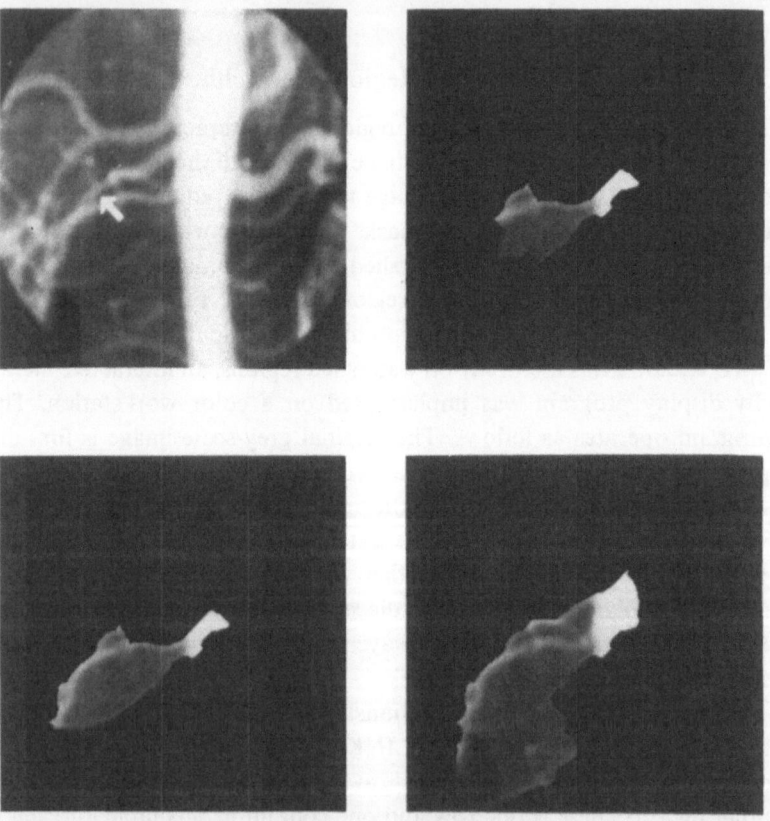

FIGURE 5.15. A DSA image (top left), a selected watershed region (top right), and higher scale parent regions (bottom left and right).

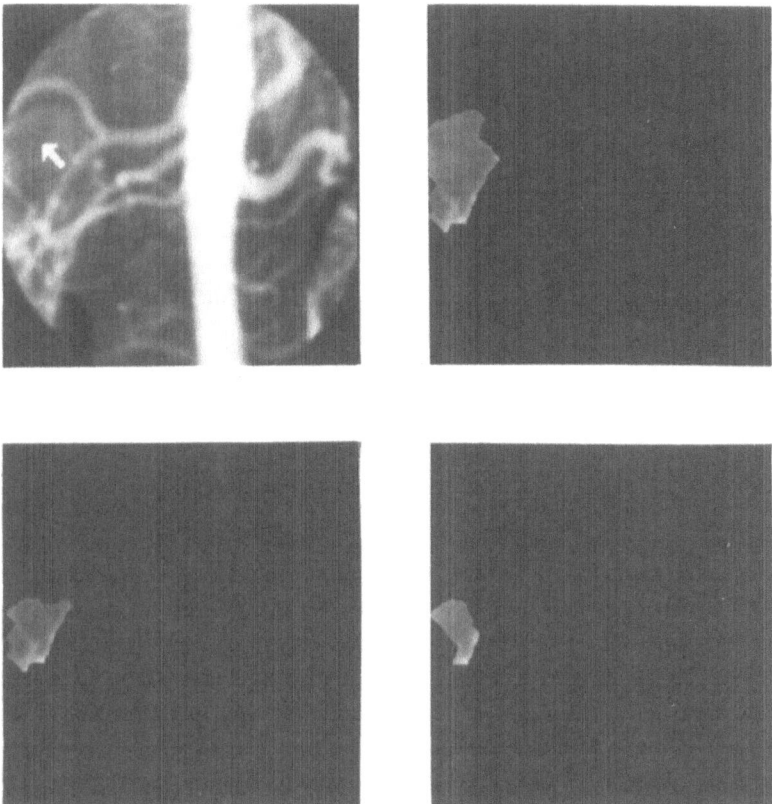

FIGURE 5.16. A DSA image (top left), a selected high scale watershed region (top right), and lower scale children regions (bottom left and right).

The row of the hierarchy table corresponding to the parent region is then scanned to identify the set of regions which annihilate into the parent at or below the blurring level required to cause the annihilation of the selected region. The union of these regions is then used to generate a display mask to select the portion of the original image to display. Thus, the parent of the selected region is displayed together with all of the children regions of the parent which have also annihilated into the parent at this scale. This process can be repeated by clicking the right button again. This provides a very useful visualization of the parent-child relationships in the watershed hierarchy (see Figure 5.15).

To lower the scale of the set of regions being displayed, the user clicks the "lower scale" button on the mouse. Since many children can annihilate into a single parent, there may be several ways to go down in the hierarchy tree. Instead of trying to select one of these lower scale alternatives, the numerical value of the current annihilation scale is simply decremented. Then the display process described in the previous paragraph is used to identify the appropriate lower scale children regions to be used to generate a display mask. The corresponding pixels of the original image are then displayed. This scale lowering process provides a very useful visualization of the annihilation order of regions in the watershed hierarchy (see Figure 5.16).

5.4.4. Associating Scale with Watershed Boundaries

After visually inspecting the watershed hierarchy to verify that it is sensible, the next task towards imposing a quasi-hierarchy on IAS sheets is associating scale information with the individual curve segments of the watershed boundaries. With this measure of importance for each ridgetop and valley-bottom in the image, it is possible to estimate the scale of each IAS sheet and impose a quasi-hierarchy on these sheets. One way to determine the scale of watershed boundaries is to interpret watershed boundaries as water barriers which disappear when adjacent watersheds annihilate into each other. Thus if region A annihilates into region B at scale 3, all boundary points which have both A and B as neighbors should be labeled with scale 3. By continuing this process for all of the annihilations between adjacent regions recorded in the hierarchy table, the majority of the watershed boundary points in the image will be labeled by scale (see Figure 5.17a).

The remaining unlabeled boundary points correspond to the special situation where two adjacent regions do not annihilate directly into each other. To handle this situation, the hierarchy data file is searched to find the lowest (smallest) scale watershed region which is a parent of both of these regions. The scale of the boundary between these regions is then determined to be the highest scale required for these two regions to annihilate into the parent region. For example, if in Figure 5.17b region A annihilates into region C at scale 5 and region B annihilates into C at scale 3, the scale of the boundary between A and B is equal to 5. This corresponds to the lowest scale at which water originally in region A will mix with water from region B.

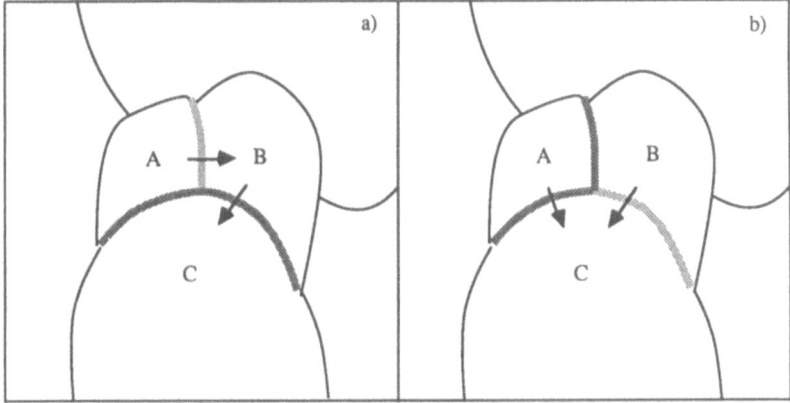

FIGURE 5.17. Associating scale with watershed boundaries. In case a) region A annihilates into B before region B annihilates into C. In case b) region B annihilates into C before region A annihilates into C.

The algorithm for associating scale with watershed boundary pixels involves

1. scanning the watershed region from left to right and from top to bottom to detect changes in region number,
2. using the methods described above to identify the scale of the boundary between these two adjacent regions, and
3. recording this information in the output image.

To reduce the computation time required to identify the scale of watershed boundaries, this information is calculated once on demand and also stored in a table for future reference. Once this process is complete, the scales of all watershed boundaries are recorded in an output image.

Since intensity is proportional to scale in this image, displaying this grey-scale image gives an indication of the importance of individual ridges and courses in the original image. For images of blood vessels, the watershed boundary segments which describe the tops of major blood vessels in an image are labeled with higher scale than those segments corresponding to smaller blood vessels (see Figure 5.18). Thus, the desired scale relationship between these image structures is captured by the scale of watershed boundaries. In abdominal CT images, this relationship is more difficult to illustrate because such images have few ridge-like

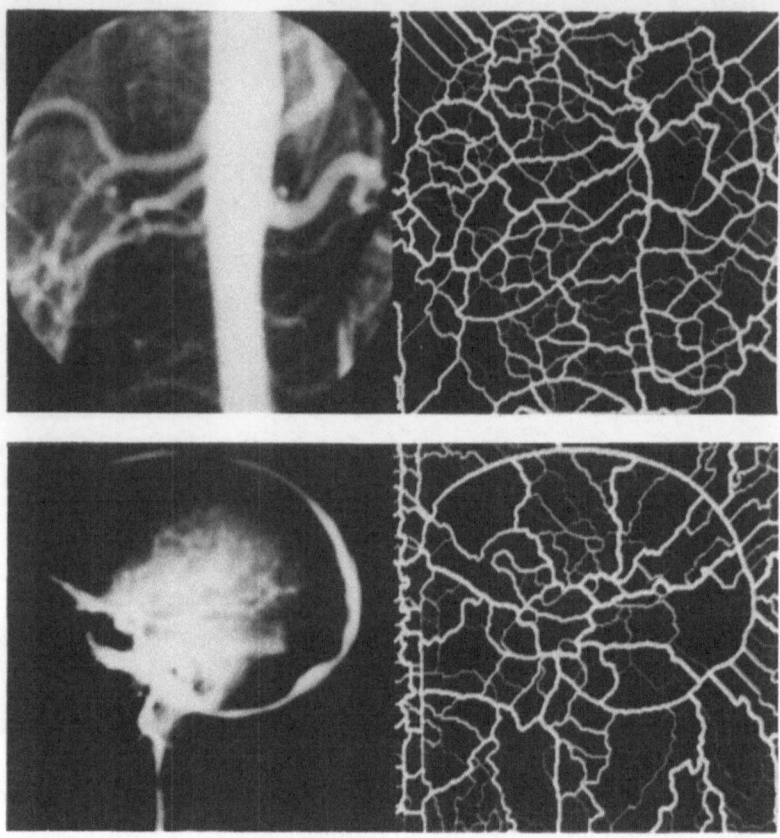

FIGURE 5.18. Watershed boundaries for two DSA images: a renal arteriogram (top left) and a carotid arteriogram (bottom left). Brightness in the corresponding watershed boundary images (top right and bottom right) corresponds to boundary scale.

anatomical structures. However, the relative scale of image structures in CT images is still apparent in the scale of these region boundaries.

5.4.5. Imposing a Quasi-Hierarchy on IAS Sheets

With the multiresolution watershed boundaries calculated above, it is now possible to estimate the scale of individual axis sheets and impose a quasi-hierarchy on the components of the IAS. Unlike vertex curves, there is not an exact correspondence between IAS sheets and watershed boundaries. There are two issues here, the spatial distance between watershed boundaries and their associated IAS end curves, and the one-to-one relationship between these structures. Axis sheets which connect intensity extrema have IAS end curves which follow ridge tops and course bottoms. When these ridges and courses are sharp and narrow, their end curves correspond very closely with watershed and hilltop boundaries. In other situations, there may be some distance between these curves. For example, if a ridge is wide and rounded, the location of the level curve extrema defining the IAS end curves may not correspond with nearby watershed boundaries. More seriously, there may be IAS sheets describing small ridges on the side of a water basin which have no corresponding boundaries. Thus, there may be fewer watershed boundaries than IAS end curves. In an attempt to overcome these difficulties, we have implemented several heuristics for associating watershed boundary scale with individual IAS sheets.

Because the image regions associated with each IAS sheet have already been computed, this information can be used to select the set of watershed boundaries which overlap each axis sheet. By calculating either the mean, median or mode value of the scale of the selected boundary points, it is possible to obtain some measure of the scale of each IAS sheet. In the blood vessel images studied with this technique, many of the blood vessel regions have scales which appear to be sensible, while others are assigned scales which are either too high or too low (see Figure 5.19). The number of boundary points along the ridge-top or valley-bottom outnumber the boundary points associated with sub-ridges or sub-courses in the region. Thus, these simple statistical measures often give an accurate reflection of the annihilation scale of the IAS sheet. To display this information, each image pixel is labeled with intensity proportional to the scale associated with its corresponding IAS sheet. White is used for high scale and black for low scale.

One problem with this heuristic approach is that IAS sheets may occasionally be assigned an incorrect scale. This is because the statistical measures described above are only approximate measures for determining the scale of an IAS sheet based on the scale of watershed boundaries "nearby" the IAS sheet. When the relative scales between adjacent sheets are maintained, these assignment errors are not a major problem. Unfortunately, there are cases where major image structures are given low scale

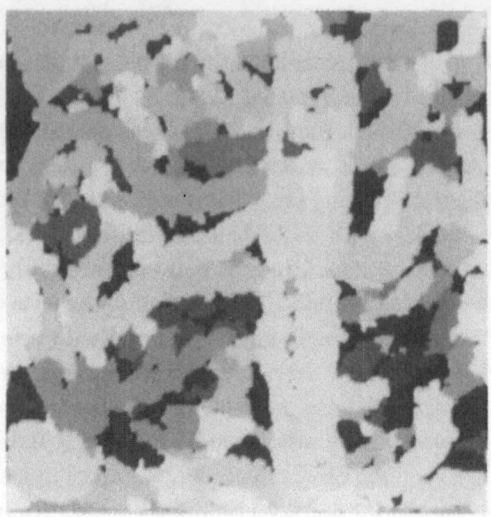

FIGURE 5.19. Scale information for individual IAS sheets for a DSA image based on the mean value of the scale of watershed boundary points.

values. One solution to this problem is to use interactive tools to manually reassign higher scales to these regions.

Determining the parent-child relationships between IAS sheets is the second half of the process of imposing a quasi-hierarchy on IAS sheets. Unlike intensity extrema and their associated watershed regions, the identification of which watershed boundary annihilates into another is not easily determined. Each watershed boundary is a curve segment which separates two watersheds and is connected at the endpoints to two other watershed region boundaries. When a boundary annihilates, it is not obvious how it should be related to these two adjacent boundary segments. Should it be the child of only one of these boundary segments or both? Hence, identifying unique parent-child relationships between IAS sheets via multiresolution watershed boundaries remains an open problem.

One approximate solution to this problem is to use the relative scales of IAS sheets calculated above, and the adjacency of IAS sheet regions in the image to record the "most likely" parent-child relationships between

IAS sheets. This can be accomplished by relating each IAS region to all adjacent regions of higher scale. Thus, each IAS sheet can have many children and many parents. Some of these relationships are visually or semantically sensible while others are not. As a consequence, this approximate quasi-hierarchy must be manually corrected using an interactive tool for editing the parent-child relationships between image structures.

5.5. Discussion

The IAS is much more difficult to follow through scale space than originally anticipated. This is principally because the individual components of the IAS are surfaces in three dimensions which can be arbitrarily connected. Attempting to compute these surfaces simultaneously across resolutions and following their annihilation directly is too computationally expensive to be effective. By focusing on the vertex curves which are associated with the end curves of these IAS sheets, this problem is reduced to following the multiresolution behavior of curves in two dimensions, and relating the derived vertex curve structure back to the original IAS sheets. Because these curves can also be arbitrarily connected, and their topology changes as blurring proceeds, attempts to implement of this approach have also proven unsuccessful.

By focusing on the annihilation of intensity extrema and their associated watersheds under resolution reduction, it is possible to assign scale to the boundaries of these watershed regions. Using an empirical relationship between these watershed boundaries and IAS sheets, the task of assigning scale to individual IAS sheets can be accomplished. Unfortunately, this does not impose a satisfactory quasi-hierarchy on axis sheets, and user intervention is required to obtain an accurate representation of the quasi-hierarchy induced on the IAS by image simplification.

This situation should be remedied by either improving the theory relating watershed boundaries and the IAS (and extending the corresponding implementation) or by solving the problem of following vertex curves through scale space. The latter approach holds the most promise since the theory is already well developed. Perhaps some of the techniques used by Bergholm [Bergholm, 1987] or Baker [Baker, 1988] to follow edges through scale space could be applied to this task. This possibility remains to be investigated.

Until some method is devised which overcomes these problems, human intervention is required to accurately represent the relationship between image structures. While this is not ideal, it does provide a means to make use of the parent-child relationships between image structures in image segmentation and other computer vision tasks.

CHAPTER 6

Conclusions

The principal objective of our research was to extend the analysis of shape to grey-scale images. This goal was accomplished by designing and implementing a new structural shape description called the intensity axis of symmetry (IAS) and an associated curvature-based description called vertex curves. Both of these descriptions focus on properties of individual level curves of the image and combine this information across intensities to obtain representations which capture both spatial and intensity properties of shape in an image. To demonstrate the effectiveness of this image shape description, an interactive image segmentation program was implemented which identifies and displays image regions associated with individual components of the IAS. These regions often correspond to sensible anatomical structures in medical images. An analysis of the multiresolution behavior of the IAS reveals that it is possible to impose a quasi-hierarchy on IAS sheets by focusing on the multiresolution properties of much simpler geometric structures: vertex curves approximated by watershed boundaries. The next four sections expand on these accomplishments.

6.1. The Definition of the IAS

Our first contribution is the definition of the intensity axis of symmetry. This shape description is specifically designed for grey-scale images and captures both the structural decomposition of objects within images and their individual width and bending properties. The branching behavior of image structures in both the spatial and intensity dimensions is reflected in the branching of individual IAS sheets. The radius and curvature functions defined on these sheets can be used to characterize portions of IAS sheets or study the width and bending properties of image structures in detail. In addition to providing an invariant description of image structures, these two functions can be used to recreate the original image. Hence, the IAS is an image transform which captures information related to edges, corners, ridges and courses in the image, which are visually significant.

6.2. An Implementation of the IAS

Our second accomplishment is the implementation of an effective method for calculating the intensity axis of symmetry. Because the intensity dimension is incommensurate with the spatial dimensions, the IAS is defined in terms of the symmetric axis for each intensity level in the image. Methods which calculate the two-dimensional symmetry axis (SA) for some collection of level curves and then attempt to connect these SAs from level to level to obtain the IAS fail to yield satisfactory results. To provide the necessary coherence in the intensity dimension, a new method for calculating the SA at all intensity levels simultaneously was developed. This was accomplished by extending the grass fire analogy of Blum to the intensity dimension. In two dimensions, the symmetric axis is defined to be the set of quench points for a grass fire started on a level curve or an object boundary. These quench points are points where fire burning from one direction extinguishes the fire burning from another direction. To calculate the IAS, the effect of a grass fire burning in (x, y, I) is simulated. A fire is started at each level curve simultaneously and allowed to burn inward towards the quench points which define the IAS, while maintaining the structural integrity of the fire surface. To ensure that the spatial and intensity dimensions remain separate, the fire is constrained so that it does not spread between intensities. There are three important aspects to this implementation:

1. To provide the necessary coherence from one level curve to the next, the image is modeled as a surface in (x, y, I). To ensure that this surface is well behaved and converges on the quench points described above, an energy functional defined on surfaces is minimized. Our functional is an extension of the active contour model of Kass to surfaces, so it is called the active surface model. This functional includes a weighted sum of first and second partial derivatives of the surface whose weights are adjusted so the surface behaves like a flexible membrane. The functional also contains a term which reflects image symmetry and directs the surface towards the IAS. Together, these terms ensure that the active surface will converge to the IAS while reducing the number of artifacts introduced by image noise. An iterative relaxation technique is used to decrease the functional value. This technique moves each point on the active surface one step in (x, y, I) towards the IAS in each iteration. Convergence is determined when the number of points moved in an iteration falls below some predetermined threshold.

2. A function in (x, y, I) has been defined to direct the active surface (grass fire). Since the grass fire always burns away from the boundary, the

distance from each point in (x, y, I) from the nearest image point at the same intensity corresponds to burning time. When this burning time is locally maximal in the burning direction, a quench point has been reached. This distance function is calculated (and inverted) and used as the image symmetry function which attracts the active surface towards the IAS.

3. A means of identifying the portions of the IAS corresponding to individual IAS sheets has been developed. The first step in this process is identifying which active surface point quenches with which. This task is accomplished by comparing the final (x, y, I) positions of each pair of active surface points. Each point is linked with the nearest point in (x, y, I) which is not adjacent on the active surface. After this linking of involutes is complete, a region growing algorithm can be used to identify which points lie on the same IAS sheet. The key to this algorithm is identifying where IAS sheets branch, and stopping the region growing from going beyond these branch points. This is accomplished by verifying that points added to the region are adjacent to other points in the region and that their corresponding involutes are also adjacent. This technique decomposes the active surface into the branching axis surfaces which comprise the IAS.

6.3. Image Segmentation Using the IAS

Our third contribution is a method for the identification of image regions with shape-based coherence which correspond to sensible structures in medical images. The task of identifying regions of interest corresponding to anatomical (or physiological) structures in medical images is an important first step in measurement and display. When these image structures are geometrically related it is sensible to use image geometry in this segmentation process. Since the individual IAS sheets describe components in an image which are part of the same symmetrical object, the identification of image regions associated with these axis sheets yields image segments which are geometrically related. Thus, by selecting individual IAS sheets and displaying their associated image regions, ridge-like (or valley-like) image structures can be identified which often correspond to sensible objects (or parts of sensible objects) within medical images. This method for image segmentation has been implemented and demonstrated on a variety of images. A preliminary analysis of the effects of image processing on this segmentation yields the following observations:

1. With no image processing, the image regions calculated by this method correspond to portions of intensity ridges in the image (or intensity courses when the IAS of inverted images is calculated). Since few structures in abdominal computed tomogram (CT) images correspond to single intensity ridges, the regions identified by the IAS are often not as good as those provided by focusing on the annihilation of intensity extrema and the following of isointensity curves through multiple resolutions demonstrated by Lifshitz. The IAS-based image regions often correspond to parts of organs, but seldom whole organs. Worse, errors introduced in representing such circularly symmetric image structures occasionally result in IAS regions which combine parts of several organs. Hence, manual editing is required to identify regions of interest. In contrast, many structures of interest in DSA images correspond to single intensity ridges. Image segments associated with IAS sheets routinely identify whole sections of blood vessels from one branching point to another. These regions are much better than those provided by the Lifshitz approach, where very few blood vessel segments are identified.

2. In theory, global contrast enhancement via histogram equalization should not affect the IAS because the relative ordering of pixel intensities is unaffected. In practice, the image symmetry function is calculated at a finite number of equally spaced intensities. By doing global histogram equalization before this function is calculated, a more uniform approximation to the IAS is possible in the intensity dimension.

3. Local contrast enhancement via adaptive histogram equalization frequently appears to yield better segmentations of small image structures. Unlike global histogram equalization, the global relative ordering of pixels in an image may be changed considerably. Thus, large image structures and the connections between such structures may be affected by such processing. In some cases this may be beneficial. For example, when the background in an image varies smoothly from one side of the image to the other, the effect of local contrast enhancement is to emphasize the foreground relative to the background. When this background variation is not essential to the task of object identification, such processing will yield image regions which are more visually

sensible. When global intensity variation is important, adaptive histogram equalization may negatively affect image segmentation by changing the global relationships between pixel intensities required to identify such image structures. The precise nature of these effects are not known.

4. Preprocessing for Gaussian blurring changes the structure of the IAS and corresponding image regions near image boundaries. Ideally image blurring should correspond to diffusion via the heat equation. For grey-scale images of finite extent, boundary effects must be anticipated and the image normalized before blurring with a Gaussian filter. Once this is done, boundary pixels have zero intensity. This changes the structure of the IAS near image boundaries. Branches no longer end abruptly at the edge of the image; they gradually diminish. Because this preprocessing changes the global relationships between pixel intensities, the precise nature of the effects of normalizing for blurring are unknown.

5. Calculating the IAS for edge strength images provides a robust means for edge detection which can be used to identify regions of interest in medical images. Because edges in typical medical images correspond to narrow ridges in gradient magnitude images, the IAS sheets which describe these ridges can be used to identify all or part of the boundary of image structures. These edges provided by this method are coherent due to the coherence of the underlying IAS for these regions. Therefore, applications which focus on object boundaries also benefit from edges identified by the IAS.

6.4. Multiresolution Analysis of the IAS

Our fourth accomplishment is an analysis of the multiresolution properties of the IAS. Blurring simplifies the image and its corresponding IAS-based segmentation. As an image is blurred, the number of intensity extrema generally decreases, causing the topology of level curves to simplify. Since the number of axis sheets is related to the number of intensity extrema, the number of IAS sheets also decreases with blurring. At the same time, the connectivity of these sheets also simplifies. Since small or low contrast image structures tend to annihilate early under blurring, the degree of image blurring required to annihilate image structures provides an indication of their scale. When importance is related to the particular combination of size and contrast that leads to a particular annihilation sequence, image blurring can be used to eliminate undesirable image features before an image segmentation based on the IAS is calculated. Hence, the image regions obtained from a blurred image will correspond to more global structures in the image. Detailed analysis of the multiresolution properties of the IAS yields the following observations:

1. There is a one-to-one correspondence between vertex curves defined by level curve curvature extrema and the individual branches of the IAS. Furthermore, these vertex curves can be easily calculated at any resolution by blurring the original image, calculating the partial derivatives of the blurred image up to the third order, substituting into an expression for the directional derivative of level curve curvature, and searching for the zero crossings of this function. The problem of following these vertex curves to annihilation through scale space and associating scale to their corresponding IAS sheets has not been solved.

2. There is an empirical relationship between watershed boundaries and the tops of IAS sheets which can be used to assign an estimate of scale to each IAS sheet and generate a quasi-hierarchy on IAS sheets. The scale of watershed boundaries can be determined by calculating a multiresolution hierarchy on intensity extrema in the image and their associated watershed regions. The heuristic for associating the scale of these watershed boundaries to IAS sheets yields only approximate results and the resulting quasi-hierarchy on IAS sheets contains parent-child relationships which are not always visually or semantically sensible. Hence, this quasi-hierarchy must be manually edited to reflect the proper parent-child relationships between IAS sheets, or the applications which use this information must be made robust to these approximation errors.

6.5. New Research Directions

While much has been accomplished by this research, there are many interesting questions which remain to be investigated. First, several problems were identified during the implementation of the IAS which should be addressed. Second, these general shape description techniques could be extended to other image analysis tasks. The remainder of this section identifies these research directions.

1. The active surface model is based on the minimization of a functional involving a linear combination of first and second partial derivatives of the surface. While satisfactory weights for these partial derivatives have been identified, the "best" weights for these terms, if an optimum exists, are unknown. Nonlinear combinations of these derivatives are also potential candidates for the active surface functional. The combinations that produce the desired active surface behavior while remaining invariant to changes in coordinates are unknown. Both of these questions are important and should be addressed. Improving the functional used for the active surface could yield better approximations to the IAS and may also reduce the computational effort required. Because the active surface is a general tool for providing coherence across one-parameter families of curves, improvements in the active surface model will be beneficial in situations requiring such coherence.

2. Minimizing a surface functional is difficult and computationally expensive. The gradient descent algorithm we implemented yields excellent results, but the small step size in each iteration of the method causes two problems. First, it slows the convergence rate of the active surface. More seriously, the active surface could potentially converge on a local minimum rather than a global solution. One minimization algorithm which addresses both of these problems is *simulated annealing* [Kirkpatrick, 1983; Geman, 1984]. This method uses large step sizes early in the minimization to avoid local minima and decreases the step size as the number of iterations increase. This ensures that high quality results are obtained in reasonable time. How simulated annealing could be integrated into the active surface model is unknown. The potential speed improvements of this minimization approach make this alternative worthy of investigation. Since many other problems are posed in this regularization framework, the results of this investigation will have wide application.

3. Better methods are needed to identify the active surface regions associated with individual IAS sheets. The two region growing algorithms obtain satisfactory results but are rather complex and computationally expensive. The basic information used by these methods is that two adjacent pixels on the active surface whose involutes are also

adjacent belong on the same IAS sheet. It would seem that this information could be used to devise an efficient region merging technique to grow all maximal regions simultaneously and thereby partition the active surface. Since this is one of the slowest steps in the process of calculating the IAS, this possibility should be investigated as an alternative to present methods. If existing region merging methods are not suited to this task, this problem presents an interesting opportunity to extend the capabilities of region merging techniques.

4. The problem of following discrete curves and surfaces to annihilation through scale space requires some mechanism which provides coherence in digital images. The active surface model used to simultaneously calculate the symmetric axis at all intensity levels is not adequate for computing arbitrary surfaces in the scale domain because it is not designed to handle changes in curve topology. Perhaps the self-organizing active contour segments used by Zucker to identify edges in an image [Zucker, 1988] could be extended to surfaces to meet these requirements. With such multiresolution following tools, the desired quasi-hierarchy on IAS sheets could be calculated and used to direct top-down or bottom-up shape analysis applications. Solving the problem of providing coherence in these complex situations will provide a tool which should be useful for computer vision applications such as motion analysis.

5. The effects of image processing on shape description are very complex and need to be studied within a solid theoretical framework. What is needed here is an understanding of the shape deformation introduced by image change. By focusing on smooth deformations of shape, a family of shape descriptions could be defined and used to understand the effects of image processing. This framework could also be used to study properties of shape in time-varying images. Because these one-parameter families of shape descriptions are less constrained than those describing the level curves that describe a grey-scale image, the mathematics of singularity theory will be essential to this analysis [Damon, 1988; Bruce and Giblin, 1986]. Perhaps the notion of describing shape change using process grammars [Leyton, 1986] could be extended to grey-scale images and used for this task. With such tools, many unexplored aspects of image shape could be investigated.

6. The image shape properties captured by the IAS could be used for other purposes. For example, nonlocal edge properties can be investi-

gated by considering both the radius properties and intensity bending of IAS sheets. Thus, the interaction of multiple edges in an image could be investigated [Pizer, 1988]. IAS features could also be used to design image warpings which make local intensities better matched with their local scale, so that local image shape will not interfere with multire-solution analysis in these neighborhoods [Pizer, 1988]. It may also be possible to identify other visually important image features (such as corners) using the IAS. These possibilities remain to be investigated.

7. The black-on-white and the white-on-black descriptions of an image must somehow be combined. The description of image shape in terms of the IAS for the volume below the image surface provides a description of light structures on dark backgrounds, while the IAS which describes the volume above the image surface is best suited for describing dark structures on light backgrounds. These two IAS structures both provide a complete description of the image (either can be used to recreate the image), so each image structure can be described in two ways. The problem of identifying which IAS should be used to describe which image structures remains open.

8. The notion of investigating grey-scale shape by focusing on the shape of one-parameter families of intensity level curves could be generalized and applied to images of higher dimension. For example, the shape of structures in three-dimensional grey-scale images could be studied via the family of three-dimensional symmetric axes [Nackman, 1982] describing the isointensity surfaces defined by this intensity function. By defining three-dimensional regions associated with components of the resulting IAS structure, shape-based segmentation of three-dimensional medical images should be possible. These three-dimensional image regions should be very useful for volume rendering applications which require the identification of regions of interest and for medical applications (such as diagnosis and treatment planning) which require the analysis of structures within three-dimensional images.

Bibliography

[Agin, 1972]
Agin, G.J., *Representation and Description of Curved Objects*, Ph.D. Dissertation, Stanford A.I. Lab, AIM-173, October 1972.

[Arnold, 1984]
Arnold, V.I., *Catastrophe Theory*, Springer, Berlin, 1984.

[Babaud, 1986]
Babaud, J., Witkin, A.P., Baudin, M., and Duda, R.O., "Uniqueness of the Gaussian Kernel for Scale-Space Filtering", *IEEE PAMI*, Vol. 8, No. 1, January 1986, pp. 26–33.

[Baker, 1988]
Baker, H.H., "Surface Reconstruction from Image Sequences", *Proceedings of the Second International Conference on Computer Vision*, Tampa, FL, December 1988.

[Ballard and Brown, 1982]
Ballard, D.H. and Brown, C.M., *Computer Vision*, Prentice Hall, 1982.

[Bergholm, 1987]
Bergholm, F., "Edge Focusing", *IEEE PAMI*, Vol. 9, No. 6, November 1987, pp. 726–741.

[Binford, 1971]
Binford, T.O., "Visual Perception by Computer", *Proceedings of the IEEE Systems Science and Cybernetics Conference*, Miami, FL, December 1971.

[Blicher, 1985]
Blicher, A.P., *Edge Detection and Geometric Methods in Computer Vision*, Ph.D. Dissertation, Stanford University, STAN-CS-85-1041, February 1985.

[Blom, 1988]
Blom, H., "Geometrical Description With a Jet Space Upon a Multi-resolution Base", *Internal Report*, Department of Medical and Physiological Physics, University of Utrecht, 1988.

[Bloomberg, 1988]
Bloomberg, S.H., *The 3D Symmetric Axis as a Shape Classifier*, Ph.D. Dissertation (draft), University of North Carolina at Chapel Hill, 1988.

[Blum, 1974]
Blum, H., "A Geometry for Biology", *Annals of the New York Academy of Sciences*, Vol. 231, April 1974, pp. 19–30.

[Blum and Nagel, 1978]
Blum, H. and Nagel, R.N., "Shape Description using Weighted Symmetric Axis Features", *Pattern Recognition*, Vol. 10, 1978, pp. 167–180.

[Bookstein, 1986]
Bookstein, F.L., "From Medical Images to the Biometrics of Form", *Internal Report*, Center for Human Growth and Development, University of Michigan, 1986.

[Brady and Asada, 1984]
Brady, M. and Asada, H., "Smoothed Local Symmetries and their Implementation", *MIT A.I. Memo 757*, February 1984.

[Brooks, 1981]
Brooks, R.A., "Symbolic Reasoning Among 3D Models and 2D Images", *Artificial Intelligence*, 17, 1981, pp. 285–348.

[Bruce and Giblin, 1986]
Bruce, J.W., Giblin, P.J., "Growth, Motion and 1-Parameter Families of Symmetry Sets", *Proceedings of the Royal Society of Edinburgh*, 104A, 1986, pp. 179–204.

[Burt, 1983]
Burt, P.J., and Adelson, E.H., "The Laplacian Pyramid as a Compact Image Code", *IEEE Trans. on Communications*, Vol. 31, No. 4, 1983, pp. 532–540.

[Burt and Hong, 1981]
Burt, P.J., Hong, T.H., and Rosenfeld, A. "Segmentation and Estimation of Image Region Properties Through Cooperative Hierarchical Computation", *IEEE SMC*, Vol. 11, No. 12, December 1981, pp. 802–809.

[Canny, 1984]
Canny, J.F., "Finding Edges and Lines in Images", *MIT A.I. Memo 720*, 1983.

[Castleman, 1979]
Castleman, K.R., *Digital Image Processing*, Prentice Hall, 1979.

[Cayley, 1859]
Cayley, A., "On Contour and Slope Lines", *The London, Edinburgh, and Dublin Philosophical Magazine and J. of Science*, Vol. 18, No. 120, October 1859, pp. 264–268.

[Coggins, 1988]
Coggins, J.M., Cullip, T., Pizer, S.M., "A Data Structure for Image Region Hierarchies", *Internal Report*, Department of Computer Science, University of North Carolina at Chapel Hill, 1988.

[Crowley and Parker, 1984]
Crowley, J.L. and Parker, A.C., "A Representation for Shape Based on

Peaks and Ridges in the Difference of Low-Pass Transform", *IEEE PAMI*, Vol. 6, No. 2, March 1984, pp. 156–170.

[Cullip, 1989]
Cullip, T., *Personal Correspondence*, Department of Computer Science, University of North Carolina at Chapel Hill, February 1989.

[Damon, 1988]
Damon, J., "Local Morse Theory for Solutions to the Heat Equation", *Preliminary Announcement*, Department of Mathematics, University of North Carolina at Chapel Hill, 1988.

[Dill, 1987]
Dill, A.R., Levine, M.D., and Nobel, P.B, "Multiple Resolution Skeletons", *IEEE PAMI*, Vol. 9, No. 4, July 1987.

[Gauch and Pizer, 1988]
Gauch, J.M., and Pizer, S.M., "Image Description via the Multiresolution Intensity Axis of Symmetry", *Proceedings of the Second International Conference on Computer Vision*, Tampa, FL, December 1988.

[Geman, 1984]
Geman, S. and Geman, D., "Stochastic Relaxation, Gibbs Distributions, and the Bayesian Restoration of Images", *IEEE PAMI*, Vol. 6, 1984, pp. 721–741.

[Ginsburg, 1977]
Ginsburg, A., *Visual Information Processing Based on Spatial Filters Constrained by Biological Data*, Doctoral Dissertation, University of Cambridge, England, 1977.

[Kass, 1987]
Kass, M., Witkin, A., Terzopoulos, D., "Snakes: Active Contour Models", *International Journal of Computer Vision*, 1, 1987, pp. 321–331.

[Kelly, 1971]
Kelly, M.D., "Edge Detection by Computer Using Planning", *Machine Understanding 6*, B. Meltzer and D. Michie (Eds.), Edinburgh University Press, Edinburgh, 1971.

[Kirkpatrick, 1983]
Kirkpatrick, S., Gelatt, C.D., Vecchi, M.P., "Optimization by Simulated Annealing", *Science*, Vol. 220, 1983, pp. 671–680.

[Koenderink, 1984]
Koenderink, J.J., "The Structure of Images", *Biological Cybernetics*, Vol. 50, 1984, pp. 363–370.

[Koenderink, 1987]
Koenderink, J.J. and van Doorn, A.J., "Representation of Local Geometry in the Visual System", *Draft Report*, University of Utrecht, 1987.

[Leyton, 1986]
Leyton, M., "Smooth Processes on Shape", *Draft Report*, Harvard University, February 1986.

[Lifshitz, 1987]
Lifshitz, L.M., *Image Segmentation using Global Knowledge and A Priori Information*, Ph.D. Dissertation, University of North Carolina at Chapel Hill, TR87-012, 1987.

[Marr and Poggio, 1980]
Marr, D., Poggio, T., Hildrith, E., "Smallest Channel in Early Human Vision", *J. Opt. Soc. Am.*, Vol. 70, No. 7, July 1980, pp. 868–870.

[Maxwell, 1870]
Maxwell, J.C., "On Hills and Dales", *The London, Edinburgh, and Dublin Philosophical Magazine and J. of Science, 4th Series*, Vol. 40, No. 269, December 1870, pp. 421–425.

[Morse, 1934]
Morse, M., and van Schaack, G.B., "The Critical Point Theory Under General Boundary Conditions", *Annals of Mathematics*, Vol. 35, No. 3, July 1934, pp. 545–571.

[Nackman, 1982]
Nackman, L.R., *Three-Dimensional Shape Description using the Symmetric Axis Transform*, Ph.D. Dissertation, University of North Carolina at Chapel Hill, TR81-016, 1982.

[Nackman, 1984]
Nackman, L.R., "Two-Dimensional Critical Point Configuration Graphs", *IEEE PAMI*, Vol. 6, No. 4, July 1984, pp. 442–450.

[Nevatia and Binford, 1977]
Nevatia, R., and Binford, T.O., "Description and Recognition of Curved Objects", *Artificial Intelligence*, Vol. 8, No. 1, 1977, pp. 77–98.

[Pizer, 1986]
Pizer, S.M., Oliver, W.R., Gauch, J.M., Bloomberg, S.H., "Hierarchical Figure Based Shape Description for Medical Imaging", *NATO ASI Mathematics and Computer Science in Medical Imaging*, 1986.

[Pizer, 1987]
Pizer, S.M., Oliver, W.R., and Bloomberg, S.H., "Hierarchical Shape Description Via The Multiresolution Symmetric Axis Transform", *IEEE PAMI*, Vol. 9, No. 4, July 1987.

[Pizer, 1987b]
Pizer, S.M., Amburn, E.P., Austin, J.D., Cromartie, R., Geselowitz, A., Greer, J., ter Haar Romeny, B., Zimmerman, J.B., "Adaptive Histogram Equalization and its Variations", *Computer Vision, Graphics, and Image Processing*, Vol. 39, 1987, pp. 355–368.

[Pizer, 1988]
Pizer, S.M., personal correspondence, Department of Computer Science, University of North Carolina at Chapel Hill, February 1989.

[Poston and Stewart, 1978]
Poston, T., and Stewart, I.N., *Catastrophe Theory and its Applications*, Pitman Publishing Ltd., London, 1978.

[Richards and Hoffman, 1985]
Richards, W. and Hoffman, D.D., "Codon Constraints on Closed 2D Shapes", *Computer Vision, Graphics, and Image Processing*, Vol. 31, 1985, pp. 265–281.

[Robson, 1983]
Robson, J., "Frequency Domain Visual Processing", *Physical and Biological Processing of Images*, OJ Braddick and AC Sleigh, ed., Springer-Verlag, 1983.

[Rosenfeld, 1979]
Rosenfeld, A., *Picture Languages: Formal Models for Picture Recognition*, Academic Press, 1979.

[Rosenfeld, 1984]
Rosenfeld, A., "Axial Representations of Shape", *Center for Automation Research, CAR-TR-102*, December 1984.

[Rosenfeld, 1984b]
Rosenfeld, A., *Multiresolution Image Processing and Analysis*, Springer-Verlag, Berlin, 1984.

[Shani, 1980]
Shani, U., "A 3D Model Driven System for the Recognition of Abdominal Anatomy from CT Scans", *TR-77*, Computer Science Department, University of Rochester, May 1980.

[Smale, 1967]
Smale, S., "Differentiable Dynamical Systems", *Bull. Amer. Math. Soc.*, Vol. 73, 1967, pp. 747–817.

[Soroka, 1976]
Soroka, B.I., and Bajcsy, R.K., "Generalized Cylinders from Serial Sections", *Proceedings of 3rd IJCPR*, November 1976, pp. 734–735.

[Soroka, 1979]
Soroka, B.I., *Understanding Objects from Slices*, Ph.D. Dissertation, Dept. of Computer and Information Science, Univ. of Pennsylvania, 1979.

[Thorpe, 1979]
Thorpe, J., *Elementary Topics in Differential Geometry*, Springer-Verlag, 1979.

[van Dam, 1988]
van Dam, W.J.M., "The Behavior of Noise in the Gaussian Derivative Model", *Internal Report*, Department of Medical and Physiological Physics, University of Utrecht, 1988.

[Wang, Wu and Rosenfeld, 1981]
Wang, S., Wu, A.Y., and Rosenfeld, A., "Image Approximation from Grey Scale Medial Axes", *IEEE PAMI*, Vol. 3, No. 6, November 1981, pp. 687–696.

[Wilson, 1979]
Wilson, H., and Bergen, J., "A Four-Mechanism Model for Threshold Spatial Vision", *Vision Research*, Vol. 19, 1979, pp. 19–32.

[Witkin, 1983]
Witkin, A., "Scale-Space Filtering", *Proceedings of International Joint Conference on Artificial Intelligence*, Karisruhe, 1983, pp. 1019–1022.

[Young, 1986]
Young, R.A., "The Gaussian Derivative Model for Machine Vision: Visual Cortex Simulation", Department of Computer Science, General Motors, *GMR-5323*, July 1986.

[Yuille, 1983]
Yuille, A.L., and Poggio, T., "Scaling Theorems for Zero-Crossings", *MIT A.I. Memo 722*, June, 1983.

[Zimmerman, 1981]
Zimmerman, J., Entenman, G., Fitzpatrick, M., Whang, J., "V Shell Reference Manual", *Internal Report*, Department of Computer Science, University of North Carolina at Chapel Hill, 1981.

[Zucker, 1988]
Zucker, S.W., Chantal, D., "The Organization of Curve Detection: Course Tangent Fields and Fine Spline Coverings", *Proceedings of the Second International Conference on Computer Vision*, Tampa, FL, December 1988.

Index